Twelve Lessons to Open Classrooms and Minds to the World

Fernando M. Reimers, Dr. Robert Adams Jr. and Kristen Shannon

With the NEA Foundation Global Learning Fellows

Kimberley Amen, Deborah (Debbie) Anderson, Heather Anderson, Jessica Anderson, Terri Anderson, Jeremy Aten, Erin Austin, Norman Ayagalria, Anuradha (Anu) Bajpai, Anna Baldwin, Brett Bigham, Deborah Bohn, Monica Bryant, Karyn Burgess, Carah Casler, Donna Cuyler, Vasiliki (Betsy) Dardeshi, Jeanne Del Colle, Shayne Dove, Chelsea Edge, Andrea Eisenberger, Kelly Elder, Mary Eldredge-Sandbo, Sonia Galaviz, Kimberley Gilles, Emily Hatch, Craig Hendrick, Carly Imhoff, Kathy Keffeler, Angela Madsen, Michelle McClaine, Luke Merchlewitz, Sarah Merchlewitz, Michele Metzler, Julie Midkiff, Peter Mili, Michael Morasse, Ikechukwu Onyema, David Ostheimer, Alicia Pahl-Cornelius, Colleen Parker, Gina Parker, Allison Riddle, Emily Robinson, M. Hannah Rodgers, Nanette Saumier-Trax, Joan Soble, Darein Spann, Dr. Joseph (Joe) Underwood, Christa Wallace, Monica Washington Laura West, Bessie Wright, Thomas (Tommy) Young, Noah Zeichner

ISBN-13: 978-0692189030 (Universal)

ISBN-10: 0692189033

CreateSpace Independent Publishing Platform
North Charleston, South Carolina

Cover art by Troy Lipscomb Design Co.

Formatted by Kristin Foster

About the NEA Foundation

The NEA Foundation is a public charity founded by educators for educators to improve public education for all students. Since our beginning in 1969, the Foundation has served as a laboratory of learning, offering funding and other resources to public school educators, their schools, and districts to solve complex teaching and learning challenges. We believe that when educators unleash their own power, ideas, and voices, communities, schools, and students all benefit.

The NEA Foundation Board of Directors

The NEA Foundation Board of Directors is comprised of savvy strategic leaders from a diverse set of fields. The Foundation benefits greatly from their thinking, their work, and their commitment to education reform. They include:

About the NEA Foundation Global Learning Fellowship

The NEA Foundation Global Learning Fellowship is an annual, national cohort-based professional development program designed to enhance educators' understanding of global competencies. Through the Global Learning Fellowship, educators have the unique opportunity to develop the knowledge and skills to integrate global competency into their daily classroom instruction, advocate for global competency in their schools and districts, and help students to thrive as global citizens in our increasingly interconnected world.

Committed to sharing what they learn and adapting their instructional practice, Fellows have developed more than 130 free, online globally-themed lesson plans, in addition to this e-book. Find more details about the program at www.neafoundation.org

Acknowledgements

The NEA Foundation would like to thank Dr. Fernando Reimers for his many contributions to this book, providing the framework, editing content, and advice and support to produce and promote it. We also thank the 2018 Global Learning Fellows and Alumni Fellows for their contributions to the lessons presented here. Finally, we thank NEA Foundation staff, Robert Adams and Kristen Shannon for shepherding this project beginning to end.

A journey of a thousand miles begins with a single step.
— Lao Tzu

Since 2010, the NEA Foundation has been on a journey to build a robust professional development program that would help educators meet their students' need for a globally conscious education.

With growing acceptance that life is no longer exclusively defined by the local communities students are raised in, but rather by the flat world that connects us to the global community, it became clear that our support of educator professional development needed to be better aligned with the global era in which we live.

Our journey began with the forward thinking and support of John Wilson (then Executive Director of NEA), Katie Berseth (Executive Vice President, North America for EF-Education First) and Mark Nieker (former President of the Pearson Foundation). Together they envisioned a fellowship program that would provide professional development opportunities focused on global competencies for public school educators that culminated with field study experiences in different places around the world.

Early on, other creative thinkers joined the team (Alex Luther, Betty Paugh-Ortiz and Ariana Curtis), to ensure our launch year was a success. Utilizing a continuous learning approach, the Foundation learned from each subsequent year.

Fast Forward nine years later and we have grown our original light-touch professional development program into a yearlong, rigorous course on global competency and educator leadership in advancing global education. The publication of lessons tied to the United Nations Sustainable Development goals guided by our renown partner, Fernando Reimers, Ford Foundation Professor of Practice in International Education at Harvard University, reflects the substantive change in our approach.

We stand today on the shoulders of every educator who has broaden our thinking on what educators need to make meaningful change in their instructional practice, if global competencies are going to be the cornerstone of education.

We salute the Board members of the Foundation for sharing their critical thinking with us as we made the journey to now.

Finally, we commend the dedicate NEA Foundation program team as they continue to march towards excellence.

The future is watching.

Onward,

Harriet Sanford
President and CEO
The NEA Foundation

Contents

Twelve Lessons to Open Classrooms and Minds to the World
Introduction:

Fernando M. Reimers, Dr. Robert Adams Jr. and Kristen Shannon

The purpose of this book

This book is the result of a collaborative effort organized by the NEA Foundation to support outstanding teacher leaders in developing challenging curriculum aligned with the United Nations (UN) Sustainable Development Goals.

The underlying premise of this work is that one of the imperatives for schools is to provide students opportunities to develop capacities that empower them to identify and achieve their goals, and to join with others in advancing shared interests. Because the larger context within which schools operate changes, the requirements for participation change as well. As a result, schools must change too in order to ensure that not only are students well taught, but that they are taught what matters. In a world that is increasingly interdependent, learning to think critically about global affairs increasingly matters. Students need to learn how local and global affairs are interdependent; they need to be able to identify shared interests and to collaborate with others across national borders.

Teachers have a central role to play in helping their students develop such global awareness and understanding. To do this they must lead in creating new curriculum and new pedagogies, and out of this professional leadership they must lead broader coalitions in support of public education's role of educating cosmopolitans at a time when public schools are under siege. The capacity of teachers as professionals to rise to the imperative of a relevant public education is augmented when they do this work with the support of professional networks. Such networks connect teachers with peers, other educators and experts who can support them in the work of developing empowering curriculum and pedagogy. In doing this collaborative work, teachers develop also the essential leadership skills to exert the essential new leadership that will sustain public education into the future. This book contains the product of the collaboration of a professional network of teacher leaders in developing a basic global citizenship curriculum, consisting of one lesson per grade, from kindergarten to high school. This chapter explains the purpose of this work and the principles which guided it.

The NEA Foundation sought to build a network of teacher leaders that would empower them through the development of a global citizenship curriculum, as well as with the intent of demonstrating the potency of such an approach. The steps followed in this undertaking were relatively simple, and could be replicated at scale to provide every teacher in the United States, indeed in the world, an opportunity to engage in a process that produces collective intelligence with respect to the question of how do we empower students to improve the world, and that in so doing builds the capacity for a new form of leadership to advance public education. These were the five steps followed:

1. The NEA Foundation identified a group of exemplary teachers from each State in the United States.

2. The NEA Foundation partnered with Harvard Professor Fernando Reimers in the design and execution of developing the global citizenship curriculum presented in this book.

3. The teachers in this network were invited to participate in a professional development retreat at which they engaged with the theory and practice of global education by attending presentations and engaging in discussions about approaches to cultivating the global competencies of students. The core of this activity was a workshop where participants discussed a process to develop a curriculum aligned with the UN Sustainable Development Goals, which had been created by Professor Reimers, consisting of an interactive process of design, application, evaluation and revision of curriculum resources aligned with the UN Sustainable Development Goals, which supports professional collaboration in the creation and revision of such resources. This approach had been previously used by various groups of diverse educators resulting in the production of curriculum resources published in the trilogy: *Empowering Global Citizens[1]*, *Empowering Students to*

---

[1] Fernando Reimers, Vidur Chopra, Connie Chung, Julia Higdon and E.B. O'Donnell. *Empowering Global Citizens*. 2016. Columbia, SC. CreateSpace.

Improve the World in Sixty Lessons[2] and *Learning to Collaborate for the Global Common Good*[3]. Such resources have been well received by a large number of educators around the world, and translated and published to various languages, including Arabic, Italian, Mandarin, Portuguese and Spanish. Some of these resources where made available to participants for study prior to the workshop.

1. At the workshop organized by the NEA Foundation, participants, structured in small groups per grade, then developed a first prototype of a lesson plan per grade, from kindergarten to high school, aligned with some of the UN Development Goals. This prototype was then reviewed by the group, using the rubric feature later in the text, for feedback that would increase the horizontal alignment of those resources across grades, as well as the vertical alignment of those resources within each grade. Those resources were then uploaded in a shared online platform which allowed all participants in the professional network to continue to study the entire curriculum and provide additional feedback.

2. Over several months, each participant in the network taught the lesson developed by their group for the particular grade in which they had worked, or worked with a cooperating teacher in the relevant grade who taught the lesson, and reconvened with their group members to evaluate their experience teaching those lessons. Based on that peer review, the lesson for each grade was revised. The curriculum presented in this publication is the result of such process of revision.

The five steps in this process reflect five key propositions:

1. Start with the end in mind to design curriculum
2. Leverage improvement networks to design curriculum
3. Learn by doing
4. Embrace the power of a problem-based education
5. Embrace the power of collaboration in diverse teams

---

[2] Fernando Reimers, et al. *Empowering Students in Sixty Lessons.* 2017. Columbia, SC. CreateSpace.
[3] Fernando Reimers, et al. *Learning to Collaborate to Advance the Global Common Good.* 2018. Columbia, SC. CreateSpace.

1. Start with the end in mind to design curriculum

The first principle is that a powerful approach to develop curriculum is to start with the end in mind. While most curriculum planning starts with direction in terms of the knowledge or competencies that it is aligned to, it seldom extends that end into a larger vision of the world that informs the selection of such competencies. As a result, while there may well be an implicit long-term vision that provides direction to the competencies which guide the development of curriculum, such vision is not public, and therefore the central hypothesis which guides such curriculum ('if students gain these competencies they will be able to achieve the following') are not public knowledge, and therefore untestable. Reimers has proposed an approach which makes the two key hypotheses which undergird any curriculum public, and therefore the subject of professional and public accountability (Reimers 2017 and 2018). Those key hypotheses are: first, that if we engage students in particular learning experiences, they will gain certain capabilities and, second, that if they gain such capabilities, they will be able to achieve particular long term results, with consequences to them and to the communities of which they are members.

The 12 lessons in this book were developed in alignment with a public, ambitious, non-partisan vision which has been endorsed by governments around the world. This is as close as we can get to a public compact reflecting humanity's shared aspiration of 'the common good'. The UN Sustainable Development Goals offer an aspirational vision of a world that is inclusive, in peace and sustainable. The 17 goals included in the framework adopted by more than 150 world leaders at the UN General Assembly in 2015 drive a series of specific targets, each spelled out in ways which are measurable. For example, Goal number 1, No Poverty, focuses on eradicating the most extreme forms of poverty from the planet. Six specific targets give concretion to this goal:

1. "By 2030, reduce at least by half the proportion of men, women and children of all ages living in poverty in all its dimensions according to national definitions

2. Implement nationally appropriate social protection systems and measures for all, including floors, and by 2030 achieve substantial coverage of the poor and the vulnerable

3. By 2030, ensure that all men and women, in particular the poor and the vulnerable, have equal rights to economic resources, as well as access to basic services, ownership and control over land and other forms of property, inheritance, natural resources, appropriate new technology and financial services, including microfinance

4. By 2030, build the resilience of the poor and those in vulnerable situations and reduce their exposure and vulnerability to climate-related extreme events and other economic, social and environmental shocks and disasters

5. Ensure significant mobilization of resources from a variety of sources, including through enhanced development cooperation, in order to provide adequate and predictable means for developing countries, in particular least developed countries, to implement programs and policies to end poverty in all its dimensions

6. Create sound policy frameworks at the national, regional and international levels, based on pro-poor and gender-sensitive development strategies, to support accelerated investment in poverty eradication actions." (Source: United Nations http://www.undp.org/content/undp/en/home/sustainable-development-goals/goal-1-no-poverty.html)

Achieving each of those targets requires specific actions which, in turn, require specific capabilities that people must have. As these global targets can only be achieved as local communities do their share, they necessarily implicate actions and choices made by many people around the world. Providing people with the capabilities to take those actions and make those choices is the task of education. In addition, engaging students with lessons aligned with real world challenges is an effective way to help them gain the capabilities to understand the world in which they live and to help improve it.

By engaging educators in the analysis of which specific capabilities are necessary to achieve these targets, and in turn discern which pedagogies and experience will help students gain those capabilities, the approach we used did more than start with the end in mind, it provided a level of transparency and professional and public accountability to the choices made in any curriculum design that are seldom available in the development of state standards or with textbooks and curriculum resources. By engaging a community of education professionals in the deliberations about how they would go from goals to targets, and from targets to capabilities and then to pedagogy, and by making those choices available to all participants in the network that developed these curriculum resources, and to those who would use them, we brought to this process of curriculum design professional and public accountability. The publication of the twelve lessons resulting from such collaboration provides an additional level of public accountability.

2. Leverage improvement networks to design curriculum

The second principle underlying the process which we followed is that the task of curriculum design, particularly when it involves domains which are novel or complex, is one that requires collaboration with colleagues. While we may cherish the idea that each teacher should be able to develop their own curriculum, in practice, the work of teaching is structured in such a way that it seriously limits how much time can be devoted to curriculum design. It is no wonder that there are many online resources designed to help teachers share curriculum and lesson and that, in practice, many teachers resort to published curriculum resources and textbooks.

The reason teachers already have created informal networks to share resources, or depend on existing resources is because the complex task of high quality curriculum development is one that benefits from economies of scale. Traditionally this has been the core competitive advantage of textbook publishers, the ability to engage large numbers of professional curriculum developers and writers in producing high quality materials that can distribute the costs necessary to fund their production across many users of such materials.

But there are limits to that conventional way to achieve economies of scale to producing instructional material, not least of which is that these resources must target some specific group of intended learners; the reason many textbooks are aligned to the standards of the largest states which have more students. One of the merits of the idea of the Common Core, a national set of curriculum standards, was precisely to enable such economies of scale in the development of high quality instructional resources.

Professional networks such as the one we constituted to develop the resources presented in this book, however, have a distinct advantage as a way to leverage collective intelligence. They can adapt dynamically to feedback resulting from rapid cycles of experimentation, and they can augment the learning resulting from similar cycles taking place concurrently in multiple settings. In this sense professional networks have an inherent potential for learning and adaptation that eludes more conventional forms of producing curriculum and textbooks.

3. Learn by doing

A third principle illustrated by the approach we adopted in constituting this professional network is that professionals must necessarily experiment as a way to themselves gain new knowledge and capacities and to create new knowledge. It may appear paradoxical that we propose an approach that provides teachers a central role in crafting knowledge on domains they may not themselves master. The reason to do this is because any curriculum is only going to be as effective as the use teachers can make of it. Strong synergies are necessary between curriculum and teacher capacities in order to sustain effective teaching practice. This means that new curriculum and new capacities need to be developed simultaneously. A very effective way to build new teacher capacities is to engage teachers in developing lessons, because this provides a performance of understanding which translates conceptual discussions into direct observable evidence of what is understood, and of potential knowledge gaps. Engaging a professional network in the review of such observable evidence is a more effective way to reach clarity into novel curriculum goals than to remain at a high level of discourse. Making emerging understandings of how to educate global citizens of a network of teachers visible with a publication of the lessons they have developed enables and invites peer review, feedback and criticism, all of which are essential for these understandings to evolve and deepen. This is what we mean by levering professional accountability in order to test the two core hypothesis of any curriculum, or of any lesson plan for that matter: a) if I do A (global education) students will learn B (global competency), and b) If students learn B they will be able and motivated to do C (achieve the UN Sustainable Development Goals).

In fact, an improvement network is simply a large laboratory that allows continuous experimentation in the quest for solutions to complex challenges. The approach we adopted is inspired in the principles of design thinking, a particularly apt methodology to develop innovative solutions to complex challenges such as the development of a curriculum that is relevant to the emerging needs of a changing context and of improvement science.

The epistemology that undergirds this principle is that professional knowledge must draw on practice; it cannot be generated in the absence of or devoid of practice. We view teaching as a profession not only in that those who practice it must master expert knowledge to guide their work, but also in the sense that those who practice it must contribute to the development of such expert knowledge. For such practice based knowledge to become professional knowledge, knowledge available to others in the profession, it must be public knowledge, not private knowledge. A professional network such as the one we have built, relying on the principles of professional and public accountability described earlier, is one way to make the knowledge that emerges from practice subject to the essential scrutiny for it to become public. Furthermore, the reliance on the principles of design based thinking and of improvement networks, provides a context for systematic experimentation and testing of the hypotheses which are implicit in any curriculum.

4. Embrace the power of a problem based education

A fourth principle embedded in the approach we followed is that some of the capacities necessary to thrive in the 21st century are best gained by engaging students with real problems and inviting students to try out solutions to those problems. Such problem and project based education draws on the traditions of progressive education developed by American philosopher, psychologist, and educational reformer John Dewey, and are consistent with current knowledge about how to support deeper learning. The use of 'grand challenges' such as those reflected in the UN Sustainable Development Goals as drivers of curriculum design is a way to align learning outcomes and pedagogy to big and ambitious problems.

5. Embrace the power of collaboration in diverse teams

The achievement of the UN Sustainable Development Goals will require unprecedented collaboration at all levels. If there is one skill all learners will need to develop is the skill to collaborate. The reliance of the resources presented in this book on collaborative project based methodologies is intended to help them develop such collaborative skills. But if teachers are to teach students to collaborate they must themselves develop their own skills to collaborate professionally. This is the reason this professional network was built as a collaborative network; we sought to provide teachers an opportunity to collaborate with colleagues, across a diverse group of American teachers.

The NEA Foundation Global Learning Fellowship. The Fellows as an improvement network.

The NEA Foundation started the Global Learning Fellowship in 2010. The impetus for establishing the program was the need to create a dynamic improvement network that would advance instructional practice in global education. The NEA Foundation firmly believes that educator voice is an essential element for designing effective education policies and practices. We noticed that educator input was missing from the emerging field of global education. The Global Learning Fellowship creates a space for educators to build their own capacity for global education while collaborating with peers from across the nation to establish educator driven perspectives on global education.

Through the NEA Foundation Global Learning Fellowship, educators develop the knowledge and skills to integrate global competency into their daily classroom instruction, advocate for global competency in their schools and districts, and help students to thrive in our increasingly interconnected world. Fellows transform their classrooms to give students a global perspective.

NEA Foundation Global Learning Fellows participate in a 12-month professional development program that includes in-person workshops, online coursework, webinars by leading experts, peer learning, and an international field study experience. After the field study, educators join a network of Global Learning Fellowship alumni who continue to explore novel ways to teach and expand global education across the public education landscape.

Why global education is essential to an education for democracy

In 1613, Juan Rodriguez (aka Jan Rodrigues and João Rodrigues), disembarked from a Dutch merchant ship named *Jonge Tobias* in Hudson Bay to trade animal skins with the local Native American population. Juan Rodriguez was an Afro-Dominican interpreter who was born in the Caribbean colony of Santo Domingo. The circumstances of how and when he came to work for the Dutch merchant ship are lost to history. When the ship was loaded and ready to return to the Netherlands, Juan decided to remain behind. He became the first non-Native American permanent settler in Manhattan.

Juan Rodriguez's pioneering settlement in Manhattan would have been lost to history if not for a commercial dispute that occurred when two Dutch ships returned to the Hudson Bay in 1614. The two rival Dutch merchant ships competed to employ Rodriguez's linguistic and commercial services. The *Jonge Tobias*, Rodriguez's original employer in 1613, arrived after the rival ship. Rodriguez's work for the rival ship created a dispute between the two merchant ships. The conflict became violent as a physical scuffle injured several crewmembers in the process. Once the two merchant ships returned to the Netherlands, the commercial dispute morphed into a legal one. The legal case produced numerous court depositions that provide the only written evidence of Rodriguez's settlement in Manhattan and his important role in facilitating Dutch and Native American trade in the Hudson Bay.[4]

The late anthropologist Michel-Rolph Trouillot designated histories like Juan Rodriguez's story as "unthinkable history."[5] These counter-narratives challenge the foundational fiction that only White European males are capable of making global history. Rodriguez's quick appearance in the historical record, before fading out of view, reminds us that many men and women of various backgrounds and origins co-constructed the colonial enterprises of post-1492 Europe. Some scholars might debate this point, arguing that Rodriguez was an anomaly, an exception to the rule. However, nearly a century before Rodriguez, Esteban Gomez (aka Estevan Gómez, Estêvão Gomes, and Stephan Gomez), an Afro-Portuguese explorer serving under the Spanish flag, led an exploration up the North American east coast as far as Canada in search of a northwest passage to the Pacific Ocean.

Others had reached Hudson Bay and parts of Canada prior to Gomez, but his expedition documented the coast more extensively than prior expeditions. His cartographic knowledge allowed the Spanish to finally recognize that the North American coast was continuous. Gomez explored and named previously unexplored parts of the New England coast.[6] Diogo Ribeiro's (aka Diego Ribero) 1527 *Padrón Real*, considered by many to be first modern scientific map, explicitly acknowledges the value of information gleaned from Gomez's voyage. The newly charted areas along the New England coast are marked on the map as "Land of Estevan Gomez" ("Tierra de Estevan Gomez).[7] Unlike Rodriguez, extensive documentation exists about Gomez's

---

[4] Anthony Stevens-Acevedo, Tom Weterings, and Leonor Alvarez Frances, *Juan Rodriguez and the Beginnings of New York City*. New York: CUNY Academic Works, 2013.

[5] Michel-Rolph Trouillot, *Silencing the Past: Power and the Production of History*. Boston: Beacon Press, 1995.

[6] J. Toribio Medina, *El Portugués Esteban Gómez al Servicio de España*. Santiago de Chile: Imprenta Elzeviriana, 1908.; Henry Harrisse, *The Discovery of North America: A Critical, Documentary, and Historic Investigation, with an essay on the cartography of the new world . . .* London: Henry Stevens and Sons, 1892.

[7] L. A, Vigneras, "The Cartographer Diogo Ribeiro," *Imago Mundi, Vol. 16 (1962), p. 78.*

broad participation in the construction and extension of the Portuguese and Spanish empires in Asia, North America and South America.[8]

Unlocking the power of America's diverse history requires more than collecting counter-narratives that reintroduce the forgotten or overlooked histories of African Americans, Asian Americans, Latinos, LBGTQs, women or the economically disadvantaged into the official story. Our nation must continue to try to live into the still unrealized pluralistic vision laid out in the founding documents. Almost 250 years after the founding of the republic, the struggle to close the gap between the American democratic idea and the practice(s) of American democracy continues. Much of American history—abolitionism; the Civil War; the end of slavery; women's suffrage; and the Civil Rights Movement—are manifestations of the eternally unfolding contestation between promise and practice. American history is replete with notable American men and women whose fame originated from the positions they took either defending the status quo of their times or agitating for a more inclusive democracy. We remember Jefferson Davis, George Wallace and Bull Conner for defending the "old" order, while we revere Frederick Douglas, Susan B. Anthony, Cesar Chavez, Martin Luther King Jr. and Fannie Lou Hamer for publically demanding the nation to fulfill its revolutionary promises.

American public education did not escape the turbulent debates about American democracy. On the contrary, the fight between the promise keepers and the status quo defenders shaped the evolution of American education. Public education played a central role in these conversations about the shape and extent of American democracy. Many consider public education to be one of the cornerstones of American democracy, signifying that schools should do more than teach grammar and arithmetic. Therefore, schools have been a key site for where the struggles over American democracy have taken place. The manifestations of this debate have varied across time, ranging from the legality of school segregation to the use of public funds for for-profit charter schools. What has been constant is the

---

[8] Nicolás Toscano Liria, "España y Portugal en la exploración de la costa atlántica de Norte América. Compilación de datos sobre Esteban Gómez," Cuadernos Hispanoamericanos, no. 788, año 2016, pp. 26-46; Luis Miguel Benito Fraile, "Esteban Gómez, Piloto de la Casa de la Contratación de la Indias," *Revista de Estudios Colombianos,* no. 13, Junio 2017, pp. 69-86.

idea of schools as mechanism of citizenship instruction; the battles occurred over what that means in practice.

Public schools are laboratories where democratic participation is taught and articulated, but they are also a public square where our citizens prepare to solve the emerging threats to democracy and free societies. Globalization is one of the key challenges currently facing us. Globalization is not a new thing. The changing characteristics of globalization, accelerated by technology, broaden its reach, thicken the connections, intensify its velocity, and exacerbate its impact. Despite the heated claims in political rhetoric, the local and the global are not mutually exclusive categories. They are complementary ones.

The current phase of globalization creates new challenges as well as presents new opportunities to solve them. The global challenges require new levels of cooperation that extend beyond the boundaries of the nation-state. Public education's earlier focus on building national identity should evolve to examine our globally linked fates. Schools can spark global problem solving approaches. The UN Sustainable Development Goals represent a device to teach a global collective conscience that does not threaten nor negate our national identities. The twelve lessons offered here reflects sample ways to use the goals in the K-12 classroom.

The Practice of Global Education and the Global Education Movement.

Aligning curriculum with a framework such as the United Nations Development Goals is clearly intended to cultivate a cosmopolitan mindset among students, to educate them as global citizens. This is indeed a global citizenship curriculum.

We see the project of educating students as a global movement which began with the dissemination of the institution of public education. This global education movement was cosmopolitan in two ways, first in that it engaged collaborations among the fraternity of educators across nations, and second in that it taught students to understand the power of such global collaborations to advance their own as well as shared challenges.

It is no accident that global public education expanded dramatically after the right to education was included in the Universal Declaration adopted by the United Nations in 1948. It was the result of the global solidarity and cooperation that was mobilized to promote global peace and stability that public education expanded its reach to include the half of the world's children who were excluded prior to the adoption of the declaration.

Similarly, the expansion of public education prior to the adoption of the Universal Declaration of Human Rights, benefited also from cooperation and exchanges across national boundaries.

Such cosmopolitan interests and efforts have always challenged, and in turn been challenged, by more parochial views of education. At present, a resurgent bigoted nationalism and isolationism, challenges global collaborations and the very aspiration of educating students to be cosmopolitan. We see such rise of intolerant nationalism, what former vice-President Joe Biden has termed 'phony populism and fake nationalism' (source https://www.nytimes.com/aponline/2018/05/24/us/ap-us-new-york-democrats.html), as dangerous to core democratic principles, such as the idea of fundamental equality of all persons or to the democratic idea that individuals must collaborate with others for the common good. These challenges to democratic values are precisely the reason to engage students with global education.

Relatedly, global education is always a pathway to develop a broader set of competencies necessary for participation in a changing world, what some have called '21st century skills' or 'deeper learning'[9]. As teachers seek new forms of learning and teaching to prepare students for the growing and more complex demands of participation in the 21st century, finding effective points of entry for pedagogical renewal is critical.

---

[9] Reimers, F. and C. Chung (Eds). *Preparing Teachers to Educate Whole Students: An International Comparative Study*. Harvard Education Publishing. (Manuscript finished and accepted, now under publication). Reimers, F. and C. Chung (Eds). 2016. *Teaching and Learning for the twenty first century*. Cambridge. Harvard Education Press.

But educational change is challenging. The notions that students should engage with real problems, or that they should do this collaboratively, for example, while hardly new, have proven remarkably difficult to translate into new pedagogical approaches that have scaled to serve all students. Global education, insofar as it is largely absent in many schools, provides a convenient point of entry for pedagogical renewal, in a way that does not directly threaten established school cultures, but that can gradually fundamentally modernize instruction.

A new leadership for public education

The institutions of public education are under attack by the same forces, which attack democracy and human rights. Sustaining public schools will require the same effective leadership as sustaining democracy will. Teachers and their organizations have an important role to play in leading a broad based movement in support of public schools, as many are doing today in various states around the United States.

If it is to successfully mobilize a democratic movement of supporters, such leadership must focus on the needs of the learners, of all learners, in a rapidly changing world. That is to say, such leadership must be at the core about the professional practice of the educator, and not just about bread and butter issues. Building this leadership will require new approaches, which should start with intellectual leadership about learning and teaching. The professional network we have built is one form to build professional leadership where teachers engage with the difficult and complex challenge of reinventing curriculum and pedagogy in order to serve students and prepare them for a rapidly changing world.

In doing this work in community, these teacher leaders also are developing the skills necessary for collaboration and for collective leadership. As the process these teachers followed included reaching out to colleagues in their schools and persuading them to experiment with the new lessons and resources included in this book, this experience provided a form of leadership development that cultivated the development of the skills needed to exercise influence without authority, relying on professional knowledge and on a commitment to an open process subject to professional and public accountability.

In translating the result of such work into a publication, this process takes the leadership development of the participants in this network one-step further, into allowing them to extend the reach of their influence by making public the knowledge created by expert practitioners so that it can be of use to others.

In this way this process has taken the participants in this network from leaders as producers of curriculum to leaders of a broader movement for curriculum renewal, and eventually, for the renewal of public education. This is the core of a broader effort to cultivate a new kind of leadership in support of public education at a time when it is under siege by the forces of bigotry and intolerance.

Kindergarten Lesson Plan

<u>Lesson Plan Title: Individualized Mindfulness and Self-Regulation Plans for Young Learners</u>

Designers: Bessie Wright, Julie Midkiff

Summary and Rationale: It is important for students to be able to self-regulate emotions and feelings. With this regulation, students can learn the ability to focus mind and body to better engage in instruction and discourse. In addition, as a teacher, you can lead students in a discussion about how children around the world face stressful situations or how students work through the problems they face in their lives?

Grade: Kindergarten

Time Frame: 30 minutes (repeated three times before assessed)

Subjects: This can be integrated into any part of the academic day and done as whole group or individually as needed.

Instructional Goal: The competencies that students will address <u>Work and Mind Habits B:</u> Identify different cultural perspectives through which to think about problems. *Work and Mind Habits 3*:   Understanding individual cultural variations within groups. Work and Mind 5: Present results of independent research in writing, orally and using media. Students will gain skills in mindfulness, which is the moment-by-moment awareness of one's thoughts, feelings, bodily sensations, and surrounding environment. Students will practice mindfulness techniques such as breathing, meditation, repetitive drawing, and/or stretching. They will have the opportunity to then develop their own mindfulness routine that can best help them overcome various obstacles and challenges that they may encounter throughout the school day.

Standards: UN Sustainable Development Goal Number 3: Good Health and Well-Being. Students will gain competencies in self-regulating their behavior by designing their own individualized mindfulness plan that they will share with their teacher and their fellow peers.

Understanding: Students will gain an understanding that self-regulation is important and there are a variety of means in which to learn to self-regulate feelings/emotions.

Essential questions:

1. How can you, refocus your energy feelings or emotions when dealing with a behavioral obstacle?
2. Can you independently create and use a technique to help you accomplish this?
3. How do children in different parts of the world experience stress and work through dealing with stress in their lives?

Student Learning Objectives: Students will be able to identify a mindfulness technique to help self-regulate emotions, energy, focus independently and share their own individualized mindfulness plan with their teachers and their fellow peers.

Assessment: The students, using mindfulness techniques, will be able to create an exercise/breathing routine that helps self-regulate and/or de-stress feelings/emotions. Students will need to be able to describe their self-regulation routine and plan with the teacher and be able to share their plans with other students in the class. Students will then be asked to record how many times throughout the school year they used their self-regulation plan. At the end of the school year, with the assistance of the teacher, students will complete a self-reflection conversation and be able to create "I can" statements when describing their self-regulation plan.

Sequence of Activities: Read *Noisy Nora* by Rosemary Wells. Afterwards ask students to identify ways in which she handles frustrations. Create a T-Chart to record the identified ways. Then ask students to identify other ways they could have handled. Teachers can then introduce a series of mindfulness activities such as regulated breathing, calming exercises, repetitive drawing, or stretching/physical activities that promote students being able to calm and self-regulate their own behavior when encountering problems and/or obstacles in the classroom.

Resources for teachers:

YouTube Videos

- Relaxing Music for Children of all ages. Perfect for quiet time, meditation, Yoga and also for nap time and night time sleeping. This video is a resource to aid young children to unwind with calming and relaxing Music.
  https://www.youtube.com/watch?v=erYQyGHC7fQ
- Mindfulness Meditation for Kids: Breathing Exercises and guided meditation for children.
  https://www.youtube.com/watch?v=Bk_qU7l-fcU
- The Listening Game: Cosmic Kids Zen Den for Mindfulness
  https://www.youtube.com/watch?v=uUIGKhG_Vq8
- Mindfulness Meditation for Children
  https://www.youtube.com/watch?v=yYQKF-9poLM

Websites:

- Asia Society
- "How Mindful Meditation Changes Lives" by Matt Schiavenza
  https://asiasociety.org/blog/asia/how-mindful-meditation-changes-lives
- Access to more videos and articles
  https://asiasociety.org/globalsearch?term=mindfulness
- Positive Psychology
- 25 Fun Mindfulness Activities and Exercises for Children and Teens
  https://positivepsychologyprogram.com/mindfulness-for-children-kids-activities
- Left Brained Buddha- 10 Ways to Teach Mindfulness to Kids
  https://leftbrainbuddha.com/10-ways-teach-mindfulness-to-kids/
- Blissful Kids Mindfulness Toolbox for Children
  https://blissfulkids.com/mindfulness-toolbox-for-children/

Pictures and articles of students in various cultures engaging in mindfulness activities:

- https://www.theatlantic.com/education/archive/2015/08/mindfulness-education-schools-meditation/402469/
- https://www.theatlantic.com/education/archive/2014/01/should-schools-teach-kids-to-meditate/283229/

- https://www.theatlantic.com/education/archive/2013/10/teach-kids-to-daydream/280615/
- https://www.health.harvard.edu/mind-and-mood/relaxation-techniques-breath-control-helps-quell-errant-stress-response
- http://www.stretch-n-grow.co.uk/exercise-is-crucial-to-help-school-childrens-brain-power/

I use ClassDojo in my classroom. Here is an example below:

- https://www.youtube.com/watch?v=r6CPzyqCff0

Videos of mindfulness activities:

- https://www.youtube.com/watch?v=CvF9AEe-ozc
- https://www.youtube.com/watch?v=shR8DLyOkcg
- https://www.youtube.com/watch?v=SpjWb9teKSY
- https://www.youtube.com/watch?v=LpU942GrNX0
- https://www.youtube.com/watch?v=kYQl0YUj-Oc (funny)
- https://www.youtube.com/watch?v=A47zwWsjXgs

Children's Book Resource List:

- *No, David!* by David Shannon
- *A Bad Case of the Stripes* by David Shanon
- *Pinkalicious* by Victoria Kann
- *Alexander and the Terrible, Horrible, No Good, Very Bad Day* by Judith Viorst
- *Thunder Cake* by Patricia Polacco
- *I Was So Mad* by Mercer Mayer
- *Sometimes I'm Bombaloo* by Rachel Vail

A kindergarten student at Bradley Elementary, Mount Hope, West Virginia drawing spirals as part of her self-regulation plan (Julie Midkiff, Art Teacher and NEA Foundation Global Fellow).

A kindergarten student at Bradley Elementary, Mount Hope, West Virginia practicing meditation as part of her self-regulation plan (Julie Midkiff, Art Teacher and NEA Foundation Global Fellow).

1st Grade Lesson Plan

Lesson Plan Title: A Day in the Life

Designers: Michael Morasse, Kimberley Amen, David Ostheimer

Summary and Rationale: This lesson aims to provide students with a deeper understanding of how their lives may be similar and different than those from students in other countries. An extension activity also demonstrates how people from the same country may have very different experiences. This lesson serves to provide an opportunity for students to appreciate the diversity of lifestyles in another country.

Grade: 1

Time Frame: 30 minutes (optional 30-minute extension activity)

Subjects: English/Language Arts (ELA), Social Studies

Instructional Goals: 1. Intercultural Competency

> A. Interpersonal Skills ii. Demonstrate empathy toward other people from different cultural origins

> B. i. Curiosity about global affairs and world cultures

Standards: UN Sustainable Development Goal Number 15: Life on Land

Understanding:

- Students will learn that the world is a big place full of many different people who live their lives in a variety of ways.
- Students will develop an awareness that their lives are similar, but also different than those who live in South Africa.
- Students will learn more authentic portrayals of life in Africa. Students will be provided examples that may be counter to stereotypical representations of life in Africa (e.g., Africa is not all lions and elephants, etc.)
- An extension activity provides the opportunity for students to learn that people that live in the same country may lead very different lives from one another.

33

Essential questions:

1. How are my experiences the same and/or different than those of children in South Africa?
2. What is a community?
3. Who lives in our community?
4. What is a home?
5. How can maps help us locate something?

Student Learning Objectives:

- Given a world map, students will be able to identify the location of South Africa.
- Given a Venn diagram, students will be able to describe the similarities and differences of their lives and the life of the student presented in the read-aloud text.
- For the extension activity, given a completed Venn diagram, students will be able to describe the similarities and differences of the lives of two children from South Africa.

Assessment:

- Students will collectively complete a Venn diagram.
- Students will use a Venn diagram as a graphic organizer to complete a short writing project. Students will describe the similarities and differences of their lives and the life of the student presented in the read-aloud text.
- Students will be assessed through conversation about what they expected to find in Cape Town and what Ashraf actually saw. Venn diagram showing the similarities and differences between our community and Cape Town.
- For the extension activity, students will use a Venn diagram as a graphic organizer to complete a short writing project. Students will describe the similarities and differences between the two children described in the books.

Sequence of Activities:

- Opening Activity/ Motivator:
  - Pair up students. Have them share with their partner what they already know about Africa. Call on a few students to share their partner's (or their own) answer and record them on the board.
- Map Activity:
  - Using Google Earth, a globe or a map, have students identify North America, the United States, their state (and town/city if appropriate).
  - Ask if anyone knows where Africa is. Find Africa and then South Africa on the map. Then locate Cape Town. What is similar and different about Cape Town's location and your location?
  - If Cape Town is in South Africa, do you think we will find the things that we talked about in our opening?
- Read-Aloud:
  - Read the book <u>Somewhere in Africa</u> by Ingrid Mennen. Discuss what Ashraf found. Did he find what you thought he would? What is different from our ideas? What is the same? Think about where you live. What does Ashraf see that you might see? What is different? What surprised you?
- Venn diagram:
  - Fill out a Venn diagram with differences and similarities between your community and Ashraf's community.
- Writing Activity/ Assessment
  - Using the Venn diagram, have students write about the similarities and differences between their community and Ashraf's community. A sentence starter may be used (Our communities are the same because… Our communities are different because…)
- Optional Extension:
  - Read <u>The Herd Boy</u> to the class and discuss the similarities and differences between Agraf's experiences in <u>Somewhere in Africa</u> and Malusi's.
  - A Venn diagram could be created to guide the discussion.

○ Discuss if the two communities in the books show the Africa that the students expected. Were they different?

Resources for teachers:

- Google Earth
- <u>Somewhere in Africa</u> by Ingrid Mennen
- <u>The Herd Boy</u> by Niki Daly
- <u>Material World</u> and <u>What I Eat</u> by Peter Menzel
- <u>Venn diagram Templates</u>

2nd Grade Lesson Plan

<u>Lesson Plan Title: A Bioblitz for Global Curiosity</u>

Designers: Gina Parker, Carly Imhoff, Heather Anderson

Summary and Rationale: Students will first develop their curiosity by asking questions about the habitat they live in, with a focus of the animals and plants they see or discover outside. Students will collect data representing the diversity of plants and animals found locally. Students will use observations and reasoning skills to collect data that answer questions related to the biodiversity of animals and plants found in different habitats throughout the world. Students also develop their curiosity by asking questions about what role humans play in negatively or positively impacting the biodiversity in their community. Students will brainstorm together in small groups utilizing the engineering design process: *Ask, Imagine, Plan, Create, Improve* with the goal of developing actions they can take to prevent biodiversity loss that negatively impact the plants and animals found in the habitats in which they live.

Grade: 2

Time Frame: 1 - 2 weeks daily, depending on the breadth of work and engagement of the students. For example, if their work develops into a larger project-based lesson, students may work collaboratively with the greater community/local environmental organizations on a project that positively impacts the biodiversity of plants and animals found in habitats in which they live.

Subjects: Science, Global Learning, Social Studies, Mathematics, ELA

Instructional Goal: Develop intercultural competencies, specifically the intrapersonal skill of curiosity about global affairs, the diversity of global habitats and world cultures.

Standards: UN Sustainable Development Goal Number 15: RI.2.1, IG 1.B.i, 2.MD.D.IA.2, K–2–ETS1–1

Understanding: Students will utilize Ask and Answer questioning skills to develop relevant questions based on the biodiversity of plants and animals found in habitats in which they live. Students will compare and contrast the biodiversity of plants and animals found in their habitat with the biodiversity of plants and animals found in habitats globally.

Essential questions:

1. What plants and animals live near you?
2. What plants and animals do you think live far away from you?
3. Why aren't there more types of plants and animals near you?
4. How do humans impact the variety of plants and animal species found near you?
5. What characteristics do the plants and animals have that give clues to where they live?

Student Learning Objectives:

- Students will learn to identify differences in the plants and animal species found locally.
- Students will be able to observe, count, record data of the plants and animals found in a given plot. If feasible, have students contrast different plots, e.g., one that is more woodsy and one that has a bunch of cement.
- Students will be able to develop questions about the biodiversity found in other habitats globally.
- Students will be able to create an action plan to prevent biodiversity loss of plants and animals.

Assessment: Teachers can use a simple T-chart as a pre-assessment with the topic questions: What do plants need? What plants are found near you? What do animals need? What animals live near you? The essential questions can be used in whole group discussions to monitor student progress. Using a variety of formative assessments for understanding will provide teachers an opportunity to make any needed adjustments to the lesson. Teachers can use exit tickets as a quick check-in, or the Think/Pair/Share method to assess their progress and understanding. Using the same simple T-charts above at the end of the lesson will show their growth and at what level they met their learning goals.

Sequence of Activities:

1.   Students will identify biodiversity where they live. Have your students conduct their own bioblitz. A bioblitz is when a team of scientists and citizen scientists count as many unique species of plants and animals as they can in a given time frame. To make this less overwhelming for students, have the students use hula hoops to create plots. Each student will lay a hula hoop outside on the ground. Then have each student count each unique plant or animal that they can identify in the hula hoop. Students can record their data using observational drawings to differentiate plant and animal species. Then gather back as a class to calculate the total amount of unique species. As a class, have the students develop questions that they have about biodiversity in other habits globally. Use the students' curiosity and questions to modify the activity in step 3.
2.   Depending on technology and capacity, have the students investigate their questions by either researching with online and text resources or by virtually collaborating with a class in a different area or country and comparing the classes' bioblitz data.
3.   Have the students develop plans/projects in order to prevent biodiversity loss of plants and animals in their community. Use examples from UN Sustainability Goal Number 15.

Conclusion: Circle the students up to discuss what they learned about the plant and animal species found in their habitat, compared with the plant and animal species found in other habitats globally, and how humans impact the biodiversity of plants and animals where they live. If the students want to take action to protect biodiversity, they could write a letter to UNESCO about why a certain habitat deserves protective status. This is also a good way to introduce students to the work UNESCO does. In addition, students can research who/what local organizations they can contact in order to present their bioblitz findings and ask additional questions of how they can make a positive impact on the plants and animals found in their community.

Resources for students:

- If you need help identifying species of plants and animals, you may want to look into iNaturalist.org which uses crowdsourcing to identify species.
- An additional resource is a short video highlighting an annual bioblitz which takes place at the Whiterock Conservancy in central Iowa. The video was created by IPTV as a part of their "Iowa Outdoors" series. It is informative and relevant for students who live in central Iowa. https://youtu.be/IK7AQDxVg3E

Resources for teachers: If you need an example of a bioblitz in another country, you can find resources about a bioblitz in Malaysia here:

- jason.org/bioblitz

3rd Grade Lesson Plan

Lesson Plan Title: Working for Water

Designers: Monica Bryant, Allison Riddle, Emily Hatch

Summary and Rationale: This lesson aims to support students in forming a deeper understanding of the barriers to accessing clean water sources by children around the world.

Grade: 3

Time Frame: 60-90 minutes, best if done in 2 sessions

Subjects: English Language Arts, Social Studies, Science

Instructional Goal: Goal 6: Clean Water and Sanitation

Standards: UN Sustainable Development Goals Number:

1.A.ii Demonstrate empathy toward other people from different cultural origins

1.B.i Curiosity about global affairs and world cultures

3.A.iv. World geography, including the different areas of the world, what unites them, what differences exist, and how humans have changed the geography of the planet.

Understanding: Students understand that not everyone accesses water in the same ways and understand why access to clean water is important.

Essential questions:
1. Why do kids need clean water?
2. What barriers do kids face when trying to access clean water?

Student Learning Objectives: Using background knowledge on how animals get water in different areas of the world, students will be able to identify ways that kids around the world obtain clean water and express empathy for those who do not have accessible clean water. Students will be able to compare their own experiences with water to kids in other parts of the world.

Assessment: As a pre-assessment, teachers can use a Venn diagram and have students select a part of the world and compare/contrast how they get access to clean drinking water with kids from that area of the world. Students must have a minimum of three examples, with one being a barrier to accessing clean water. Formative assessments throughout for each activity, such as think/pair/share, thumbs up/down, turn and talk, exit tickets, etc. will provide teachers with how students are doing throughout the activities. As a post-assessment, teachers will repeat the pre-assessment, in order to see growth and to what degree students met the learning objectives.

Sequence of Activities:

Opener: (Connect to previous learning about animals.) Describe how animals in various habitats get water: savanna, desert, rainforest, woods, forest, arctic, grasslands, wetlands, caves. Compare to the UNICEF Water map (https://www.unicefusa.org/water-map) - identify as a class where those different habitats are on the globe and look at how people obtain water in those areas. What UNICEF projects are active? Explore the map, looking at how people and animals get water in different parts of the world.

Activity 1: Read *Three Stories About How Clean Water Saves Kids' Lives* (https://www.unicefusa.org/three-stories-about-how-clean-water-saves-kids-lives) as a class. Locate those three countries on the UNICEF map.

Discuss:

- What were the kids' lives like before they had clean water?
- How did their lives change as a result of getting clean water?
- How did they get clean water?

Optional extension: Look at *A Cool Drink of Water* and connect to how kids in various cultures use and conserve water.

Activity 2: Read The Water Princess and discuss the struggle Princess Gie Gie and her mother encounter when obtaining clean water.

Use turn-and-talks during the story to give students a chance to articulate their understanding of the book. Use questions such as:

- Why is it difficult to get water for Gie Gie?

- What other places would have the same challenges?
- What are Gie Gie and her mother thinking?
- How can you tell Gie Gie and her mother are challenged?
- Why do you think Gie Gie and her mother need water?
- How is Gie Gie's experience getting water different from yours?

Activity 3: Teacher shares how he/she gets water in her own home.

Have students write a personal narrative about how they get water in their own homes, what they use clean water for, and how often they need to access water.

Have students compare this to how kids in another area in the world get water. Or, the teacher shares an example of a time when he/she had a difficult time getting clean water.

Then have students write about a time when they had a difficult time getting clean water, for example, while camping, on a road trip, or while at an event. Have students compare this to how kids in another area in the world get water.

Closing: Students share their writing (in partners, or to the class). Discuss how students in the class had similar or different experiences each other. Review why clean water is important, and what barriers prevent access to clean water in the world.

Optional action step: Have your class participate in UNICEF fundraising activities or share personal narratives about water with people in power (congressmen, representatives, or local businessmen) urging empathy and compassion for the world in lawmaking and charitable donations.

Resources for students:

- https://www.unicefusa.org/water-map
- https://www.unicefusa.org/three-stories-about-how-clean-water-saves-kids-lives
- *A Cool Drink of Water* by Barbara Kerley
- *The Water Princess* by Susan Verde

Resources for teachers:

- https://www.unicefusa.org/water-map
- https://www.unicefusa.org/three-stories-about-how-clean-water-saves-kids-lives
- National Geographic photos: drinking water around the world
- A Cool Drink of Water by Barbara Kerley
- The Water Princess by Susan Verde

4th and 5th Grade Lesson Plan

Lesson Plan Title: Water is Life

Designers: Terri Anderson, Norman Ayagalria, Carah Casler, Sonia Galaviz, Christa Wallace, Laura West

Summary and Rationale: Students will understand the need for clean water as a human right across cultures, and how citizens of other cultures might or might not have access.

Grades: 4,5

Time Frame: 3 days or 3 parts, each 3-4 hours per part

Subjects: Economics, Geography, Literacy, Math, Politics, Science, Social Justice, Social Studies.

Instructional Goal: Intercultural Competency

- 1B.i. Curiosity about global affairs.
- 1B. ii. The ability to recognize and weigh diverse cultural perspectives.
- 1B. iii. An understanding on one's identity, of other's identities, and of how other cultures shape their own identities.
- 1B. iv. The ability to recognize and examine assumptions when engaging with cultural differences.
- 1B. vi. Understanding and appreciating cultural variations in basic norms of interaction, the ability to be courteous and the ability to find and learn about norms appropriate in specific settings and types of interaction.

Standards:

- UN Sustainable Development Goal Number 6: Clean water and Sanitation
- UN Sustainable Development Goal Number 10: Reduced Inequalities
- UN Sustainable Development Goal Number 11: Sustainable Cities and Communities

Understandings:

- Quantity and quality of water is different for different people due to geographical, political and economic reasons.
- Water inequality in this country and other countries.
- How do gender inequalities affect how water is provided to certain communities?
- How do economics impact access to water?
- What can I do to conserve water so that it is accessible to all?
- Essential questions:
- What does access to water look like in your culture and other cultures/societies?
- What can YOU do to affect change in the world?

Essential questions:

1. What does access to water look like in your culture and other cultures/societies?
2. What can YOU do to affect change in the world?

Student Learning Objectives:

- Students will measure their personal water use and determine ways to conserve water. They will use various resources such as https://www.swfwmd.state.fl.us/conservation/thepowerof10/, and others listed in the resource section to learn the average water usage when we flush a toilet, shower, brush our teeth, etc.
- Students will create a three-day water usage timeline to find daily average water consumption in their households.
- Students will compare their access to water to those people in other parts of the world.
- Students will make a written plan, pledge to conserve their average water usage, and encourage their families to do the same through a written letter that also documents the amounts of water used in various household activities.

Assessment Method: Rubric Checklist

A variety of formative assessment methods will be used based on assignments, classroom discussions, and student partner/group work. The assignments of assessment include a home water use calculation checklist, comparing personal home water use to other developing countries, and inquiring community members about water use as a human rights issue.

Part 1: 3-4 hours

Objective	Assignment/Task	Proficient
Student is able to calculate daily water use.	Students complete daily water use calculator as homework.	Student can calculate personal water use independently.
Student is able to explain the most and the least amount of personal water use.	Students calculate which is the most and the least amount of water using a graph drafted from personal water use.	Student can explain the most and the least amount of personal water use.
Student is able to explain personal water usage can be predictable daily.	Students use daily water usage graph to compare and contrast water usage.	Student can explain their daily water usage is similar, different, or predictable.
Student is able to convert gallons to liters.	Students use a calculator to convert gallons to liters.	Student can convert gallons to liters independently.

Part 2: 3-4 hours

Objective	Assignment/Task	Proficient
Student is able to compare personal water use to other developing countries.	Students complete a Venn diagram of person water use to other developing countries.	Student can explain with sufficient details of how same or different their water use is.
Student is able to empathize other developing countries pack water.	Students experience packing water with a five-gallon bucket of dirty water.	Student uses experience to explain how difficult it is to pack water daily.
Student is able to summarize interview findings.	Students interview parents about water use as human rights issue.	Student can explain or summarize their interview findings.

Part 3: 3-4 hours

Objective	Assignment/Task	Proficient
Student is able to develop ideas on how to decrease personal water use.	Students use the personal water calculator to begin decreasing personal water use.	Student can explain those ideas on how to decrease personal water use.
Student is able to generate different strategies to assist other developing countries access potable water.	Students work in groups to create brochures, posters, a movie, or other mediums to explain their ideas for clean accessible water.	Student can explain their ideas by their choice of project.

Sequence of Activities:

1. Class discussion on how much water we use. How many times do you use water each day? What are those activities? How many times do you flush the toilet?
2. Use daily water use template. Family interviews (see template).
3. *See "Sequence of Activities" file for direct instruction
4. Resources for students and teachers:
5. Book: Long Walk to Water
6. *Do the Green Thing* website, dothegreenthing.com, focus on climate change and creativity
7. Templates for water use
8. Sample interview questions
9. YouTube video: *Lucy Billings-Carry the Water*, various YouTube videos depicting how water is brought in to different communities. Water.org has many YouTube videos.
10. Water use by US: https://water.usgs.gov/edu/qa-home-percapita.html

Part 1

Overview: In Part 1, students will explore their own water use and calculate total water use in their home during a 24-hour period. Students will discuss findings as a class and generate questions based on their data. Extensions might include converting calculations from gallons to liters, charting water use individually or as a class in graphs, or calculating the water use of the entire family.

Opening: Discuss as a class how much water we think we use. Have students think about how many times a day they use water. What are those activities? (Examples: toilet flushing, brushing teeth, bathing, cooking, washing clothes/dishes, etc.) Students can write their initial thoughts on this discussion in their science or writing journal.

Steps:

1. After the discussion, students will take home a Daily Personal Water Use Calculator to record their water use for 1 day. Students will bring that data record back to school the next day.
2. Students will calculate their own personal water use based on the data from the template. Was it more or less than they expected? What

uses the most water? Does our water use change day to day? What would the water use look like for their whole family? For the whole classroom? Discuss at length, record in their science/writing journal.

3. Extension activities with the data from their water use template include: converting gallons to liters, graphing daily use, graphing use as a class, calculating and/or graphing a week's worth of water use, calculating their whole family's use, etc.

Conclusion: Wrapping up the discussion should include the students' takeaways from their calculations. Discuss as a class whether the students think everyone has access to limitless water. Have they ever been in a situation where their water was limited, scarce, or non-existent (e.g., camping, water was turned off, etc.)? What do they think the challenge would be if their water was limited? How would that impact their lives as they know it right now?

Part 2

Overview: In this activity, students will compare their own water use to those in developing countries. Students will experience hauling a five-gallon bucket of water and use that experience to emphasize how much water is actually used for simple tasks in their daily life. Students will document their understanding about water use, hauling water, and how this might influence their own personal water choices.

Opening: Review the Daily Personal Water Use Calculator from the previous activity. Review the discussion about experiences where the students haven't had typical access to clean water. Review as a class the first few sections of Water Facts from https://www.waterinfo.org/resources/water-facts. Discuss what this means to the students. How does this compare to their personal water use? What questions do they have? Then watch Empowering the Girl Child from the Water Project (www.thewaterproject.org). https://www.youtube.com/watch?list=PLDZXcv-5kqbcQieIrIaqkcwG1PXq3NSn1&v=1aW7fpd4GdY Discuss the video and get prepare for the water haul experiment.

Steps:

- After students have reviewed Part 1 activities, read the Water Facts, and watched the video, it is time to haul the five-gallon bucket of water.
- Students will seek to empathize with the physical hardship of hauling water for personal use. Students can carry water individually or in teams. The water haul can be done outside or in a hallway.
- Students will fill out the Water Haul reflection after the experience. Discuss as a class.

Conclusion: Students should hopefully have an "ah-ha" moment in realizing how difficult it can be to haul five gallons of water, which is all some people have for their daily water use, in developing countries. Discuss the inequality of access to safe, clean water. In the concluding conversations with the class, give some questions to consider for the following day. "Is water a human right?" "What does water mean to us?" "Why is it important?" In addition, these questions will be in the homework assignment after today. Students will interview their parent or a family member about those 3 questions.

Part 3

Overview: In this final part, students will make the connections between personal water use, water as a global right and resource, and what steps they can take to conserve/reduce their water use. Students will generate ideas for an action plan to help reduce their water use in their own home and an awareness campaign throughout the school.

Opening: As a class, review the students' interviews and what their families think about water as a human right. Review student takeaways from their own water use compared to water use in developing countries.

Steps:

1. Students can share in small groups, then as a class, their interviews about water with their family.
2. Discuss as a class what actions can be taken to address water overuse, in our homes, school, and local communities. Ideas might include: information campaign, posters, presentations to other classrooms, teaching our families, etc.

3. Develop a plan based on ideas for action. Students can work in small groups to tackle an action. (Where possible, involve the families.)

4. An extension activity would be to problem solve and develop an action plan to help developing countries' access to clean water. Examples of global initiatives can be found at http://www.shoemanwater.org/about.html, https://thewaterproject.org/,
   o https://www.classy.org/blog/5-nonprofits-make-clean-water-global-reality/, and
   o http://www.care.org/work/health/clean-water .

Conclusion: Students should feel like they have some plan of action to tackle water overuse within their own homes and school. Students can communicate with their families what steps they would like to take and work to educate the whole family about what they've learned. Students could easily develop an information campaign with their school and local community to bring awareness about water use/abuse, as well as find ways to contribute to global efforts to increase clean water access in developing countries.

Resources

Lessons:

- http://worldslargestlesson.globalgoals.org/global-goals/clean-water-sanitation/

Clean Water Initiatives:

- http://www.shoemanwater.org/about.html
- https://thewaterproject.org/
- https://www.classy.org/blog/5-nonprofits-make-clean-water-global-reality/
- http://www.care.org/work/health/clean-water
- Water crisis in in the United States (Flint, MI and beyond):
- Photos of the water crisis-

http://www.theatlantic.com/photo/2016/02/we-fear-the-water/459687/

- Taking action: https://oied.ncsu.edu/main/thinkanddo-the-flint-water-crisis/
- Water crisis and race/poverty: http://www.cnn.com/2016/01/26/us/flint-michigan-water-crisis-race-poverty/
- Lead in numerous schools across the United States: http://mobile.nytimes.com/2016/03/27/us/schools-nationwide-still-grapple-with-lead-in-water.html?referer=android-app://com.google.android.googlequicksearchbox
- Lead in NY schools: http://mobile.nytimes.com/2016/02/09/us/regulatory-gaps-leave-unsafe-lead-levels-in-water-nationwide.html
- Lead in Chicago schools: http://www.chicagotribune.com/news/ct-chicago-lead-water-risk-met-20160207-story.html
- Water.org YouTube videos about water from Kenya: https://www.youtube.com/watch?list=PLDZXcv-5kqbcQieIrIaqkcwG1PXq3NSn1&v=1aW7fpd4GdY
- https://www.youtube.com/watch?v=qfyRKOjvN3I
- https://www.youtube.com/watch?v=8STrs78yxO0
- https://www.youtube.com/watch?v=PZ6J3hUo0kE

6th Grade Lesson Plan

Lesson Plan Title: Education for All Children

Designers: Jeremy Aten, Karyn Burgess, Kelly Elder, Craig Hendrick, Nanette Saumier-Trax.

Summary and Rationale:

In this lesson, students will be exposed to impediments to receiving basic education. This will increase their empathy for and understanding of factors that prevent children from going to or staying in school. Children around the world are prevented from receiving basic education. Access to quality basic education is the single best way to combat poverty around the world.

Grade: 6

Time Frame: 60 minutes

Subjects: Advisory/Homeroom, Social Studies, English Language Arts

Instructional Goal:

1. Intercultural Competency
   (A) Interpersonal Skills.
      ii. Demonstrate empathy toward other people from different cultural origins.
2. Ethical Orientation
   (B) Commitment to basic equality of all people.
2. Ethical Orientation
   (D) Appreciation of the potential of every person regardless of socioeconomic circumstances or cultural origin.

We want our students to know that access to education is indeed a privilege that is not afforded to all children around the world and articulate obstacles to education and the implications of *not* having access to a quality education.

Standards: UN Sustainable Development Goals

- Number 4: Quality Education
- Number 5: Gender Equality
- Number 10: Reduced Inequalities

Understanding:

- Quality education is a privilege that has value and, for a variety of reasons, is not afforded to all students throughout the world.

Essential questions:

1. What are the implications of not having access to education?
2. What are some obstacles to getting an education?

Student Learning Objectives:

- By the end of the lesson, students will be able to identify one or more impediments to education and how the impediment impacts educational access. Students will name one or more possible solutions to overcome that particular obstacle.

Assessment:

- Students will write a short, individual reflection on the factors that contributed to the position of their representative. Possible prompts the teacher may provide include:

  - What did you discover?
  - What could be done to change those circumstances?
  - What are solutions to the impediments that stifled your representative's progress toward being able to earn a living wage?

Sequence of Activities:

Opener: What can education provide? Why do we encourage and provide education to students? If children are afforded quality education, they stand a much better chance of being able to earn enough money to provide for their needs.

Core Events:

- Define "living wage." This is an approximate income needed to meet a family's basic *needs*. Earning a living wage enables the working poor to achieve financial independence while maintaining housing and food security. Brainstorm in a class discussion what things would be expected if someone is earning a living wage.
- Discuss the need for people to be able to earn a living wage and things that may make that difficult.
- Divide students into 8-10 equal groups. Designate one student to receive the biography in each group. Distribute one biography (attached) to each group. Biographies will include details that would impact a child's educational opportunities. Information such as accessibility of schools and teachers, expectations place on the child other than school (for example work, food and water collection, fulfilling gender roles), and community and family support will be included.
- Read the biography together. Discuss challenges and advantages of the person whose biography they have received.
- One representative from each group goes to the front of the room. This may work better in the hallway, a gym, or outside since a wide space would be beneficial in illustrating the point. Label a starting line "Birth" and a finish line "Earning a living wage" with enough room for 15 small/normal steps. You may need to mark the length of each step to regulate student movement or else results will be very skewed.
- Representatives will line up at the "Birth" line. The teacher will read out circumstances and the students will move forward based on the directions given.

  o If your community has free access to education for you, step forward three steps.
  o If the teacher in the school in your community is well trained, step forward one step.

- o If the school in your community has books and supplies, step forward one step.
- o If your school has services to provide education for someone with your disability, step forward one step.
- o If your community has clean water easily available, step forward one step.
- o If your family does not need you to go to work to earn money to help sustain them, step forward two steps.
- o If your family and community allow people of your gender to attend school, step forward two steps.
- o If your community or country is not at war, step forward one step.

- No child should have reached the living wage finish line at this point; however, students will be dispersed unequally between the birth line and the finish line.
- Return to the classroom. Create a graphic representation of the student's positions on chart paper, the chalk board, or computer. Note inequality of opportunity and ask students to write a short reflection on what factors contributed to the representative of their group's progress toward earning a living wage.

Conclusion:

- Lead students back to the updated chart with some of the obstacles to education lifted. Lead class in a concluding discussion.
- Reflect on each participant's new position. Did anyone reach the Living Wage finish line? What else is required to bring each student to the living wage finish line (e.g., individual effort, diligence, and grit)?
- In their groups, students will create a plan to resolve some of the obstacles to their representative's ability to attend school as a means of eventually earning a living wage. In 20 minutes, students will create a plan to resolve as many of the obstacles as possible. Students will present their plan to the class and demonstrate how many steps resolving the obstacles they did would allow their representative to move forward on the chart.

Resources for teachers: Attached biographies

Read the biography you have been given thoroughly. Answer each question below based on what you have read.

Our group read the biography of _____
from _____ .

Question	Yes	No
Does your community have free access to education for you?		
Is the teacher in the school in your community well trained?		
Does the school in your community have books and supplies?		
If you have a disability, does your school have services to provide education for someone with your disability?		
Does your community have clean water easily available?		
Does your family need you to go to work to earn money to help sustain them?		
Does your family and community allow people of your gender to attend school?		
Is your community or country at war?		

Read the biography you have been given thoroughly. Answer each question below based on what you have read.

Our group read the biography of _____

from _____ .

Question	Yes	No
Does your community have free access to education for you?		
Is the teacher in the school in your community well trained?		
Does the school in your community have books and supplies?		
If you have a disability, does your school have services to provide education for someone with your disability?		
Does your community have clean water easily available?		
Does your family need you to go to work to earn money to help sustain them?		
Does your family and community allow people of your gender to attend school?		
Is your community or country at war?		

Biographies. Cut apart and distribute to groups of students. Choose the 8-10 biographies that seem most appropriate for your class. Groups should be 2-4 students.

Astur is 12 years old. She stays home to help collect water from a well that is quite a long walk. Astur will help her mother clean their home and gather wood for the cooking fire. There is a lot of work to do to keep the family going. It is common for girls to stay home like Astur. She lives in a country where only 36% of girls go to school. Each day, her brother goes off to his primary school in Mogadishu, Somalia. Her parents can only afford the school fees for one child so her brother was chosen.	Omer, 11 years old, and his family were forced to flee their home in the town of Mingkaman, South Sudan. Omer's family had raised cattle and farmed a few vegetables. Now they are spending their days seeking a safe place to stay. They are often hungry, thirsty, and lack safe shelter. Hundreds of thousands of children have been displaced in this country since violence erupted late last year. Omer had attended a school before the family was forced to escape the war but like 48.5 million children worldwide, he has left school because of war.

Chandni, 12 years old, was born in Bangladesh with cerebral palsy, a disability that limits her movement. Her family lives together in a small house. Her father's job provides them with enough money for food and water. But, she needs a wheelchair to move and special assistance to feed herself. The school in her community does not have a wheelchair ramp for her to get inside of her classroom and no one to help her with writing, feeding, or exercising her muscles. Chandni has never been to school. Around 150 million children in the world live with a disability - 80% of them are in developing countries and nine out of 10 of these children do not attend school.	Dawa, 12 years old, lives in Adonkia, Sierra Leone. Her parents have told her of war that ravaged their homeland when they were children. She knows her country has struggled with rebuilding. Things are still unsafe and the government is not providing money for water, schools, roads or police. There is no school in Adonkia to attend. Her town had tried to start a school, but they did not have a teacher; older students from other schools would try to teach. Dawa's parents decided it was not worth the money or effort to keep her in school. Some of the poorest countries in the world struggle to finance an education system for their children.

Effat, 14 years old, lives in Nigeria. She had attended school when her parents did not need her help at home. She enjoyed school and her teachers were nice. But then her father arranged a marriage for her and an older man from her village. She had to leave school and soon became pregnant with her first child. It is estimated that 15 million girls around the world are married before they turn 18. After their weddings they leave the education system and, armed with few educational skills, they and their families are more likely to live in poverty.	Danilo, 12 years old, lives in Tacloban City, Philippines. One year ago his home and much of his community was destroyed by a typhoon. His father has been unable to return to his job at a furniture factory that also was destroyed. Danilo and his family live in a make-shift structure made of plywood and canvas. It has no running water or electricity. They cook over a fire. They work to clear their home site and have begun rebuilding. It is unclear when, if ever, Danilo will be able to return to school. Unforeseen events such as earthquakes, floods and disease can derail education for millions.

Aleksi lives in Finland with his mother and father. His home is comfortable and safe. He was born deaf but received cochlear implants young with speech and educational therapy provided by his school. He was able to talk with hearing peers by the time he started primary school. He quickly learned to read with the help of a special teacher for the deaf. In Scandinavian countries, there is a strong commitment to free education for everyone at all levels. There is a 100% literacy rate.	Moise is a child worker who pans for gold at a mine in the Democratic Republic of Congo. By mid-afternoon, he is watching the clock and waiting for the home-time bell to ring. Moise must earn money to help his mother pay for their home and food. He and his mother must gather water from a river and carry it home in buckets. Like Moise, there are more than 168 million child laborers — 11% of all children in the world — who are working instead of learning. More than half of them work in farming and almost a third in the service sector.

Na Young lives in South Korea. Her parents both attended a university and have provided her with a private music and math tutor since she was four. Her parents and tutor believe she is quite intelligent and have high educational expectations for her. She attends a school near her home six days a week and is provided breakfast and lunch there. Children in her school are quite competitive for the best grades and challenge each other to improve their scores. 100% of the children in South Korea attend primary school and all of them learn to read.	Raul, 13 years old, lives in Los Angeles, California with this mother. His mother works 12-16 hours a day cleaning houses. He misses school once or two days per week to take care of his little brother and sisters when his mother does not have another babysitter. His teachers try to help him but are often frustrated with his poor attendance. That makes him dislike going to school. Raul is thinking about quitting school when he is 16 so he can get a job to help his mother pay for their apartment and food. For many Hispanics living in the United States, initial disadvantages often stem from parents' immigrant and socioeconomic status and their lack of knowledge about the United States education system, resulting in Hispanics having the lowest rates of high school and college degree attainment, which hinders their chances for stable employment. More than one-fourth of Hispanic adults have less than a ninth-grade education.

Clarissa lives in South Strafford, Vermont with her parents and three brothers. Her mother is a cashier at the grocery store in town, and her dad works as a custodian. They have a safe and comfortable home, and the school Clarissa attends has a wide variety of courses and clubs for her to choose. In elementary school, Clarissa had a hard time learning to read. Her school placed her with a reading teacher three times per week until she was caught up to her peers. Now she loves to read and frequently visits her school and local library to check out books. Clarissa also enjoys playing soccer and texting her friends.	Amira, 14 years old, lives in Saudi Arabia. Her home is safe and comfortable with bountiful food. Her family are devout Muslim who value respect and tradition. She studies very hard at school, because she would like to become a lawyer — a job now open to women in Saudi Arabia. She attends an all-girls school near her home where she lives with her mother, father and brother. The teachers in her school are all female. In Saudi Arabia primary education to high school is free available to everyone. According to UNESCO, gross enrollment for boys is 99% and 96.3% for girls.

7th Grade Lesson Plan

Lesson Plan Title: Trust Building

Designers: Debbie Anderson, Angela Madsen, Hannah Rodgers

Summary and Rationale: With the rapidly changing secondary school environment in mind, this lesson aims to support middle level tweens in developing greater trust for each other and adults. For sustainable human interaction and global institutions, this lesson aims to support middle level tweens in building trust and identifying causes of a trust breakdown

This lesson fits into the entire curriculum.

Suggested as an introductory plan for earlier in the school year/semester.

Grade: 7

Time Frame: 1 - 2 days

Subjects: Art, Literature, Social Studies, Theatre

Vocabulary: Perspective, mis/communication, trust, 'social contract,' justice, *ubuntu*

Instructional Goal: To develop a stronger disposition of trust aligned with empowering global citizens.

Restorative justice is an effective tool used to begin the healing process after a specific harm has occurred.

1B.vi. Intrapersonal skill: an appreciation and understanding of cultural variation

Standards: UN Sustainable Development Goal Number 16: Peace, Justice and Strong Institutions

Understanding: Trust and Personal Perspective

Essential questions:

1. How do people see the world differently?
2. How can discussion with others help us understand perspectives that are different from our own?
3. Restorative justice: How can we make our relationships more trusting?

Student Learning Objectives: Students will (or will be able to):

- Explain their own view of art clearly enough for another student to clearly understand their viewpoints.
- View pictures from multiple perspectives to comprehend alternatives
- Reflect on their own communication and analyze any breakdowns in communication with a partner.
- Set reflective personal goals to improve their communication practices, such as identifying a relationship to develop better.

Optional starting activity: Pass a message example
Bell ringer (log in journal): Describe a time when you were betrayed by someone or when you felt guilty for breaking trust someone placed in you.

Assessment: Students will reflect on the following questions:

1. How well did I communicate my ideas with my partner? On a scale of 1-10, how would you rate yourself and why?
2. When you did struggle to communicate, what did you do? What helped you communicate more clearly?
3. How can you use this knowledge of different perspectives to get along with others?

Sequence of Activities:

1. Gallery Walk procedures
   a. Pictures of optical illusions are spaced around the room
   b. Students are instructed to walk around the room QUIETLY and write down answers to: What do you see in each picture?
   c. Students choose a partner and go back to pictures and discuss what they see.
   d. As a class, discuss the pictures (possibly projected up).
   e. Students write in their reflection journal.
2. *Literature Tie: The Blind Men and the Elephant.*
   a. Volunteers read to class.
   b. Other volunteers silently reenact the poem/folktale.
   c. Discussion of the poem or folktale, leading to the importance of each other's perspective. (May use suggested questions from the Peace Corps.)
      https://www.peacecorps.gov/educators/resources/story-blind-men-and-elephant/
   d. Students write in their reflection journals.

Homework/Application: Reflection to set personal goal to improve their communication practices (e.g., listening, perspective taking), such as selecting someone with whom they'd like to improve trust, making a plan of action to carry out, and reviewing their progress

Extensions integrating across the curriculum:

- Socio-Emotional: peer mediation training, trust walks, journal reflection
- Math: explorations of 4D tesselations and tesseracts
- NeuroScience: receptors, optics, refraction
- Literature: *A Wrinkle in Time*, "tesseracts"
- Art: perspectives such as 1-point, 2-point, 3-point

Resources for students:

- Roza, Greg. An Optical Artist: Exploring Patterns and Symmetry. Math Tesselations.
- Maurits Cornelis Escher (1898-1972) http://www.mcescher.com/
- Sarcone, G. A. Optical Illusions. Lake Forest, CA: QEB Publishing, [2017]. Scholastic Book Fair.
- Tutu, Desmond and Mpho Tutu, The Book of Forgiving, This outlines a Fourfold Path, four steps that replace a cycle of violence with a cycle of forgiving:
  - Tell the Story
  - Feel the Feelings
  - Forgive
  - Choose to either renew or release the relationship

- Gucciardi, I. (2017). Coming to Peace: Resolving Conflict Within Ourselves and With Others. Sacred Stream Publishing. ISBN 978-0-692-70549-0   https://sacredstream.org/coming-to-peace-by-isa-gucciardi-phd/
- Hayward, K. The Year When All the Forgiving Happened: 2016. International Integrators. https://internationalintegrators.org/the-year-when-all-the-forgiving-happened-2016/

Resources for teachers:

- Amenta-Shin, Gina. Trust Game Board. TeachersGiveTeachers. Hyperdoc from Gameboard Template design by Genevieve Pacada for a more self-directed online experience. https://docs.google.com/document/d/13oIHloB4c6E7DZ48MFqt eSe5NQBIaHn0P2Vu7TN6R14/edit?usp=sharing
- Social Justice Standards. Teaching Tolerance project. The Southern Poverty Law Center. https://www.tolerance.org/frameworks/social-justice-standards
- *The Blind Men and the Elephant* Lesson. Peace Corps. www.peacecorps.gov/educators/resources/blind-men-and-elephant/.
- The 12 Principles And Power Of Empathy, Forgiveness, Definition, Research, Religious Views In Judaism, Christianity, Islam, Baha'i, Buddhism, Hinduism, Jainism, Ho'oponopono, Humanist, Relationship, Meditation Experiential Exercise
- http://www.agreenroadjournal.com/2015/08/the-12-principles-and-power-of.html
- Bar-Siman-Tov, Y. From Conflict Resolution to Reconciliation. Oxford University Press. https://books.google.com/books?isbn=0195347277
- Hamlin, J. B. (2014) The Semiotics of Restorative Justice: The Healing Garden Nurtured from the Well-Spring of Signs, Symbols and Language Int J Semiot Law 27:217–221 DOI 10.1007/s11196-013-9349-2 https://link.springer.com/content/pdf/10.1007%2Fs11196-013-9349-2.pdf
- Walker, M. U. Restorative Justice and Reparations. http://web.mit.edu/~sgrp/2007/no2/WalkerRJR.pdf

Reconciliation and Justice

- The colloquium intends to create a space for the discussion of such issues with an intercultural orientation and it seeks to explore further the dimensions of reconciliation from a philosophical perspective, particularly as interconnected with the notion of justice. https://philevents.org/event/show/16185

8th Grade Lesson Plan

Lesson Plan Title: Empathy and Natural Disasters

Designers: Michelle McClaine, Sarah Merchlewitz, Alicia Pahl-Cornelius, Brett Bigham, Anuradha Bajpai

Summary and Rationale: The aim of this lesson is to cultivate global curiosity about current events and make connections to students' lives in order to build empathy.

Grade: 8

Time Frame: 1 session with optional extensions

- Session 1: Identify natural disasters and respond with empathy
- Extension Sessions: Read additional articles; service learning ideas, Skype opportunities

Subjects: Multidisciplinary (Science, Social Studies, Literacy emphasis)

Instructional Goal: Cultivate global curiosity about current events and make connections to students' experiences.

Standards:

- UN Sustainable Development Goal Number 11: Sustainable Cities and Communities
- Intercultural Competency (A: Interpersonal Skills: 2- Demonstrate empathy toward other people from different cultural origins; B: Intrapersonal Skills: 1 - Curiosity about global affairs and world cultures)

Understanding:

- Use current events to discuss natural disaster aftermath.
- Listen to/read texts around natural disasters and human responses.
- Optional: Brainstorm potential solutions for the future of communities in disaster-prone areas after engaging in first-hand conversations and Research.

Essential questions:

1. What types of responses do humans have when faced with natural disasters?
2. Where do natural disasters happen? What is the scale?
3. Which feelings stir us to act after a natural disaster? Which feelings keep us from acting?

Student Learning Objectives:

In this lesson, students will:

- Develop awareness of natural disasters globally by marking all recent natural disaster areas shown in opening activity on a map and reading and responding to at least one article.
- Build empathy for victims of natural disasters by discussing ways to allocate resources in a small group and then reading an article on other childrens' responses to compare with one's own feelings.
- Respond to why this global issue matters by annotating the text and creating a paragraph or captioned drawing that combines understanding of ideas and feelings.
- (Optional: Encourage problem solving to address natural disasters through additional activities such as engaging with other classrooms via technology or experimenting with science concepts that lead to natural disasters, among others. See Extension section.)

Assessment:

- Map activity and stickers -- Teachers informally assess based on whether students are using all of their materials appropriately.
- Annotated article -- Teachers may use their own annotation or text coding assessment tool.
- Exit ticket and response paragraph/captioned drawing -- Teachers may use the rubric below to assess the understanding of the two main lesson objectives about *understanding natural disaster effects* and *articulating their own empathetic responses*.

	Emerging (1)	Developing (2)	Proficient (3)
Ideas Does the student engage with the information by using specific details and/or by providing a fresh perspective on the topic?			
Empathy Does the student mention the feelings that arose after reading the articles and conducting their group discussion?			

Sequence of Activities:

Opener:

Use the following link to introduce the 10 deadliest natural disasters of 2017. (Another slideshow may be used, depending on how current events change at time of implementation.) Teachers may conduct this as a whole-class activity or in small groups, if there are enough computers or tablets available.

https://www.usnews.com/news/best-countries/slideshows/10-of-the-deadliest-natural-disasters-of-2017

- Emphasize the different disasters that affect different regions of our country and the world
- Introduce the disasters through a global lens, responding to questions on vocabulary and geography as needed
- Highlight how natural disasters do not discriminate based on SES, race, religion, gender but human responses do
- Discuss what types of relief efforts are needed in the disaster aftermath

First Activity:

Note: This activity was taught in order to reinforce awareness of geography and to provide background context. It also added visual and manipulative elements for a Special Education class of one of the authors.

For this portion, students may work in small groups or pairs. Provide students with a world map per group/pair that has the countries from the slideshow labeled on the map. Give each group/pair a sheet with 10 stickers. Small sticky notes would work as well. Tell students that each sticker represents an amount of money that can be used to help rebuild a community affected by the disasters. (Example: "Each sticker is worth $1,000 that can help a country clean up, rebuild, or help care for the people after a natural disaster.") Have students discuss and decide where they will "donate" their "resources" by placing the sticker on their choice of countries on the map. Encourage students to articulate a reason for distributing their resources to each place. Let them develop their own criteria, but here are some questions to assist them:

- Do you know anyone in the affected countries?
- Do you want to help the countries with the highest death toll?
- Do you want to help the countries/regions that were hit by more than one disaster?

Have each group share their final map, showing where they distributed their "resources" and how they made their decisions. If short on time, have students summarize where most of their "resources" went and why.

Second Activity:

Read the following article independently or in small groups:

"Empathy during a natural disaster"

http://healthland.time.com/2013/01/22/how-disasters-and-trauma-can-affect-childrens-empathy/

Encourage students to use their classroom annotation protocol. One way to do it is to write down Questions, Connections, and Reactions. (See sample stems below).

- Questions: How...? I wonder...? Where...? Why...? What it...?
- Connections: I can relate to... This reminds me of...
- Reactions: This makes me think... I am surprised by...

After everyone has finished, discuss comments and reactions to the article, and check for understanding. Important points:

- Article summary
- Ask if students can see a relationship between the experiment described in the article and the map activity students did earlier.
- Was anyone surprised about the difference in the feelings and reactions of the older children versus the younger children?
- Why might their reactions be different? Do you agree with this, based on your own experience?

Conclusion:

Assign students a reading response and/or an exit ticket to gather their feedback and provide assessment data. Responses can be in written or drawn form, depending on student level and preference. (Sample response templates: https://goo.gl/epSCB8, Sample exit ticket: https://goo.gl/wJNwr5) Responses should include wording that recalls the Essential Questions, such as students' own feelings and reactions to natural disasters and the effects and scale of natural disasters.

Optional Lesson Extensions:

Should a teacher want to continue exploring causes and effects of natural disasters and the range of empathetic responses that can result, here are some suggestions of culminating projects and extensions that can be used in the classroom. Different activities require different levels of preparation and technology. For example, debating about the safety of coastal cities requires a few more articles and videos, and students could create a poster or have a debate about proposed solutions. A Skype connection with another classroom would require additional planning and initiation from the teacher as well as student background research from students before a meaningful conversation can take place. Depending on how these may fit into an existing curriculum, teachers also could narrow this list and let student groups choose their area of individual interest from the list below. Be sure to identify the UN Sustainable Development Goal(s) that corresponds with each choice.

- Analyze and compare seismograms from multiple earthquakes for the relationship between amplitude and energy.
- Organize a service learning project/fundraiser at local school to help the school(s) in the affected area.

- Debate about safety of coastal cities and propose steps for sustainability.
- Research, fundraise, and donate to someone or a group from an area hit with a disaster using a Kiva microloan.
- Activity worksheet: *What Five Things Would You Take if a Natural Disaster Was Coming?*
- Skype with a classroom where a natural disaster affected the community. Mystery Skype is also an option.
- In groups of four students select four of the eight links below to review, take notes, and discuss. Allow students the opportunity to choose the links in order to promote student agency.

  ○ Surviving a Natural Disaster: http://secretsofsurvival.com/natural-disaster.html
  ○ How to Help? - http://kidshealth.org/en/teens/natural-disaster.html
  ○ Savage Earth: Global Perspective: http://school.nettrekker.com/goExternal?np=/sections/external/web/external.ftl&pp=/sections/external/web/external.ftl&evlCode=2888564948544312mihvLf&productName=school&al=Middle
  ○ Challenge of Predicting The Earthquake: :https://app.discoveryeducation.com/learn/videos/383fcc79-12e7-4443-8073-f081f019e24e?hasLocalHost=false
  ○ Interactive Video: https://app.discoveryeducation.com/learn/player/07C6580E-D804-48F2-BC00-702B1729833F
  ○ Earthquake Triggers Tsunami: https://app.discoveryeducation.com/learn/videos/4dc053d8-a752-4777-b668-aaf963e0db07?hasLocalHost=false
  ○ https://drive.google.com/file/d/0B8gADvQRul5AdjhPUWhoa1Y0LWU2VFJqcFZlMzNvMUFxaWUw/view
  ○ https://drive.google.com/file/d/0B8gADvQRul5AX2k2Y3E0Q001WVktdXkzNTR5bFM2VG00bTdv/view

9th Grade Lesson Plan

<u>Lesson Plan Title: Ethical Analysis of Promoting Health and Well Being</u>

UN Link: http://www.un.org/sustainabledevelopment/blog/2017/09/un-health-agency-recommends-large-scale-deworming-to-improve-childrens-health/

Designers: Shayne Dove, Darein Spann, Ikechukwu Onyema

Summary and Rationale: This lesson will introduce students to ideas connected to health challenges within a population and ask them to investigate and consider the ethics of a government caring for and regulating people's health and well-being.

Grade: 9

Time Frame: One week

Subjects: Science (medicines, effects of chemicals), social studies (mapping, data), health/PE, English, math (data analysis), Business (ethics of pharmaceuticals)

Instructional Goal:

- Focus on the wellbeing of women and men. This curriculum, with a strong focus on gender equity will prepare graduates to support gender equitable policies that will support the good health of women and children.
- Target knowledge and dispositions that would support health, although in general the development of critical thinking skills and the capacity to learn will support graduates in this course in becoming effective promoters of their own health. The course also develops awareness of the importance of health and cultivates advocates for health for all.

Standards: UN Sustainable Development Goal Number 3: Good Health and Well Being

Goal 3 targets

- By 2030, end the epidemics of AIDS, tuberculosis, malaria and neglected tropical diseases and combat hepatitis, water-borne diseases and non-communicable diseases
- Support the research and development of vaccines and medicines for the communicable and noncommunicable diseases that primarily affect developing countries, provide access to affordable essential medicines and vaccines, in accordance with the Doha Declaration on the TRIPS Agreement and Public Health, which affirms the right of developing countries to use the full the provisions in the Agreement on Trade Related Aspects of Intellectual Property Rights regarding flexibilities to protect public health, and, in particular, provide access to medicines for all

Ethical Orientation

- C. Recognition of common values and common humanity across civilization streams.
- D. Appreciation of the potential of every person regardless of socio-economic circumstances or cultural originals.
- F. Commitment to supporting universal human rights, to reducing global poverty, to promoting peace, and to promoting sustainable forms of human-environmental interaction.
- H. An understanding of the role of trust in sustaining human interaction as well as global institutions and recognition of forms of breakdown in trust and institutional corruption and its causes.

Understanding:

Parasites can cause disease in humans. Some parasitic diseases are easily treated, and some are not. The burden of these diseases often rests on communities in the tropics and subtropics, but parasitic infections also affect people in developed countries.

- What are common human parasites, what are the symptoms, what is the geographic range, what is the treatment?
- What are common health requirements in the United States?
- What diseases and parasites are prevalent in regions or communities (global epidemiology of diseases)?

Essential questions:

1. What are the ethical implications of mandating health treatments?
2. Whose responsibility is it to promote people's health and wellbeing?
3. How much power should the government have and use in order to ensure "health safety"?
4. How do the standard procedures for ensuring health and safety of citizens in the United States compare with other countries?

Student Learning Objectives:

1. Students will compare and contrast the role of the UN and the World Health Organization in organizing community health initiatives for some countries. What other organizations promote health?
2. Students can identify common human parasites around the world and describe the treatments.

Assessment:

1. Using Google Slides, students will collaboratively create a fact book of common human parasites. Each student will research one parasite and provide common data about the parasite. Teacher should allow student choice in parasites but facilitate the choosing of parasites to ensure that many are covered, and all regions of the world are included. (Global extension: partner with a school in South Africa to complete the Project.)
2. Research project into (local) community ailments, causes and solutions

Sequence of Activities:

Opener:

Open by talking to students about access to clean drinking water and how access (or lack of access) could or does affect their quality of life. Provide examples of lead in water, chemicals in water, and parasites in water sources.

Activities:

Reading: UN health agency recommends large scale deworming to improve children's health. Students will closely read the document (highlight/underline key information, summarize key sections, ask questions of the text, make connections, draw conclusions), create questions to further thinking, and identify and define technical vocabulary. If teacher is unfamiliar with the close reading strategy, information can be found from the Association for Supervision and Curiculum Development (ASCD)-

http://www.ascd.org/publications/educational-leadership/dec12/vol70/num04/Closing-in-on-Close-Reading.aspx).

If students need additional guidance in close reading, they can find it here, https://writingcenter.fas.harvard.edu/pages/how-do-close-reading.

Guest speaker: Invite a speaker from the local community health agency to discuss immunization initiatives or other subject. During the presentation, students will record a list of questions for the speaker and the most important points from the presentation. After the presentation, students will ask their questions of the speaker and engage in a discussion around the most important points from the presentation. Topics for questions and discussion will vary depending on the topic of the presentation.

Conclusion: What ailments are prevalent in your community? What causes them, and what are some solutions (e.g., research project. solution oriented research)?

Resources for students:

- CDC Parasite Index A to Z: https://www.cdc.gov/parasites/

Resources for teachers:

- https://youtu.be/SAMlE68olqc

- A 12 minute documentary detailing the fight for a clean and safe environment. Patsy Oliver and FUSE led this fight to clean Carver Terrace in Texarkana, TX. This is her story.

10th Grade Lesson Plan

Lesson Plan Title: Understanding Food Security

Designers: Emily Robinson, Donna Cuyler, Erin Austin, Michele Metzler, Andrea Eisenberger

Summary and Rationale: In this lesson, students will learn about the pillars of food security and discover resources and/or organizations—locally, domestically, and internationally—that work to end hunger. Extension activities include content-specific lessons to create cross-curricular connections.

Grade: 10

Time Frame: 60 minutes

Subject: Social Studies

Instructional Goal: Students will be able to explain the pillars of food security. Students will be able to identify local, national, and international organizations that work to reduce or end hunger and evaluate the effectiveness of these organizations.

Standards: UN Sustainable Development Goal #2: Zero Hunger

3. Knowledge and Skills

   C. Economics, business, and entrepreneurship

   v. The consequences of global poverty and the agency of the poor

   E. Public Health, population, and demography

Understanding: Hunger is an issue all over the world. There are many organizations that are working to end hunger, which is one of the UN Sustainable Development Goals.

Essential questions:

1. What are the pillars of food security?

2. What effect does hunger have on our community? Our country? Our world?

3. How are different organizations within our community addressing food security? Our country? Internationally?

4. What would a world without hunger look like?

Student Learning Objectives:

- Students will demonstrate understanding of the four pillars of food security—availability, accessibility, use of food, and stability of the food supply—through journaling and class discussion.

- Students will work in pairs to document research about the work of one domestic and one international hunger relief organization.

Assessment:

Formative Assessments:

a. Students will participate in a prompted journaling activity in which they will record their thoughts on hunger and food security. The teacher will assess this activity through a journal check.

b. Students will follow a set of prompts to participate in a class discussion about food security.

c. In partner sets, students will complete one template for a domestic hunger relief organization and one template for an international hunger relief organization. They will then use a Venn diagram to compare and contrast the effectiveness of the two organizations.

d. In groups, students will research and create a hunger relief sales pitch. They will then assess their peers through voting for which sales pitch they think is the most effective.

Culminating Activity Assessment: The class will implement their hunger relief plan. The teacher will assess this activity based on the student-created action plan for the campaign.

Optional Extension Activity: students will respond to questions regarding a *Newsweek* article on the food security of the nation of Ethiopia.

Sequence of Activities:

1. Opener: Journal about hunger. Consider the following questions:

- When do you feel hungry?
- When you're hungry, how does it affect you?
- How do you define food security?

Reconvene as a class and discuss student answers to the journal prompts (if appropriate). *Option*: Create a Google Form survey to ask the hunger-related questions so that you can project the response data, and the students can discuss them while keeping their personal contributions anonymous.

"Challenging Hunger In the United States," Teaching Tolerance

(https://www.tolerance.org/classroom-resources/tolerance-lessons/challenging-hunger-in-the-united-states)

2. Introduce the concept of hunger as defined by the UN. Using the prompts below, discuss the concept of the 4 pillars of food security and how hunger exists in every nation in the world, including the United States. Explain to students that one of the UN Sustainable Development goals is to have zero hunger worldwide by 2030.

- How would you describe each of the 4 pillars of food security?
- How do hunger and limited access to food affect people?
- Who should be responsible for making sure everyone, everywhere has equal access to food?

Mercycorps.org
(https://www.mercycorps.org/sites/default/files/FoodSecuritySectorApproach.pdf)

3. Tell students that there are many organizations that are actively working to end hunger. Have students brainstorm a list of these types of organizations, first in their community, then nationally, and finally internationally. (You may need to help with this part.)

a) What can we do in our own community to end hunger? Find 1-2 hunger relief agencies in your community and log their contact information (website, email, phone number)

b) What can we do in our own country? Find 2-3 national agencies and log their contact information (website, email, phone number)

c) What can we do in the world? Find 2-3 international agencies and log their contact information (website, email, phone number)

Domestic Organizations: Part 8/page 94 Local Assistance
http://alliancetoendhunger.org/aeh-playbook/

4. In pairs, have students choose and research one domestic and one international hunger reduction organization using the template provided. They will then use a Venn diagram to compare and contrast the two organizations. (*Option*: Have each pair share their research. Use chart paper to develop a set of similarities and differences for all of the organizations researched, including the perceived effectiveness of each organization.)

Venn diagram:

https://www.canva.com/design/DAC7AXE6tk4/m_LznHmo-KpkjEf_nKpeRg/edit?layouts=&utm_source=onboarding

5. Culminating Activity

a. In groups, students choose one type of organization (local, national, or international) and prepare a "sales pitch" for their classmates in which they promote a fundraising idea for that organization based on their assessment of the organization's needs. The "sales pitch" should be 3-5 minutes long, and needs to include:

1. Name and location of the organization

2. A brief history of the organization

3. Which pillar of food security the organization works to support

4. Fundraising goal (created by the group)

5. Plan for what the hunger relief sales pitch campaign would look like, including a timeline of what activities will happen and by when. The plan needs to be SMART.

    a. Specific (simple, sensible, significant)

    b. Measurable (meaningful, motivating)

    c. Achievable (agreed, attainable)

    d. Relevant (reasonable, realistic and resourced, results-based)

    e. Time bound (time-based, time limited, time/cost limited, timely, time-sensitive)

  b. Each group will present their "pitch" to the rest of the class.

  c. The class will vote on which campaign they would like to pursue.

6. *Optional extension*: Have students read the *Newsweek* article "Solving Hunger in Ethiopia by Turning to Native Crops" and respond to the following questions:

Make a list of the common threats to food security in Ethiopia. (Remember to think of the four pillars of food security.)

Explain the solution that Tadesse Kippie and others have suggested about native crops.

Do you think the solution outlined will help to reduce or eliminate the traditional threats to food security in Ethiopia? Why or why not?

Resources for students:

- World Food Program: (https://www.wfp.org/node/359289)
- Josette Sheeran's TED Talk, *Ending Hunger Now* (https://www.ted.com/speakers/josette_sheeran)
- Learning to Give: (http://www.learningtogive.org/units/food-thought-hunger%E2%80%94around-block-around-world/making-difference-world) (includes several links to other information sites)
- Hungry Planet:

(https://menzelphoto.photoshelter.com/gallery/Hungry-Planet-Family-Food-Portraits/G0000zmgWvU6SiKM/C0000k7JgEHhEq0w)

- "Solving Hunger in Ethiopia by Turning to Native Crops *Newsweek:* http://www.newsweek.com/2014/12/26/solving-hunger-ethiopia-turning-native-crops-291558.html

Resources for teachers:

- "Solving Hunger in Ethiopia by Turning to Native Crops *Newsweek:* http://www.newsweek.com/2014/12/26/solving-hunger-ethiopia-turning-native-crops-291558.html
- Domestic Organizations: Part 8/page 94 Local Assistance: http://alliancetoendhunger.org/aeh-playbook/
- UNESCO's FAO Strategies for Improving Food Security: http://www.unesco.org/education/tlsf/mods/theme_c/popups/mod14t04s01.html
- UN Sustainable Development Goal 2: Zero Hunger: http://www.un.org/sustainabledevelopment/hunger/
- TED.com search results on hunger: https://www.ted.com/search?q=hunger
- "Challenging Hunger in the United States", Teaching Tolerance https://www.tolerance.org/classroom-resources/tolerance-lessons/challenging-hunger-in-the-united-states
- Learning To Give: (http://www.learningtogive.org/units/food-thought-hunger%E2%80%94around-block-around-world/making-difference-world) includes several links to other information sites)
- Regional Foodbank of Oklahoma: https://www.regionalfoodbank.org/uploads/docs/Activity%201.pdf
- Mercycorps.org: https://www.mercycorps.org/sites/default/files/FoodSecuritySectorApproach.pdf
- Stanford Center on Food Security and the Environment: http://fse.fsi.stanford.edu/
- Peace Corps Volunteer Information

(https://www.peacecorps.gov/volunteer/what-volunteers-do/)
(Look particularly at agriculture, environment, and health)
- "Plate Pioneerz for the Global Goals", World's Largest Lesson: http://worldslargestlesson.globalgoals.org/healthy-not-hungry-food-projects-for-the-goals/
- Green Bronx Machine: https://greenbronxmachine.org/

Template for students:

Hunger Relief Programs
Location of organization; is this domestic or international?
Name of the program and Internet address:
What is this program's method of dealing with hunger problems? (In other words, how do they help?) Which pillar of food security does this program work to address?
Who is served by this program? How many people are helped?
In your opinion, how effective is the program?

Cross-Curricular Connections (ideas to implement this lesson's goals into other classes):

- Science - Analyze the nutritional content of different food sources; evaluate the placement of food sources on an energy pyramid; assess caloric needs of individuals and how much food is needed to meet those needs; discuss farming practices that are sustainable; research the geographic sources of foods and learn about urban deserts, eating local, and other connections between ecology, sustainability, and nutrition.

- English - Pair this lesson with literature related to not having enough food, such as the memoir *Night* by Elie Wiesel or the section from Richard Wright's autobiography *Black Boy* (alternate title: *American Hunger*) that describes his lifelong struggle with not having enough to eat.

- World Languages - This lesson could be used to analyze the food security in countries where the language being studied is spoken. In an IB World Language classroom, this lesson plan perfectly fits the IB Diploma Programme's Core Topic of Global Issues.

- Art - Spread the word. Create an infographic/social media campaign that visually communicates information/research on one of the 4 objectives of the lesson. Use Picktochart , SPARK, or another app to assist in creating informational graphics. Participate in an Empty Bowls Event. Create visual representations of what a student thinks hunger/poverty looks like (both concrete and abstract variations). Use the images from *What the World Eats* as inspiration for class discussion or the students own photographic documentation of what they eat.

- AP Art History - Student research and presentations on the theme of "symbolism of food in art" using specific works that span time and geography.

- Math, Health, and Physical Education - Math classes will research average caloric *intakes* of various countries, including food-insecure countries. Physical Education students will track their caloric *output* for a week. Math classes will then compare average caloric outputs of U.S. students vs. the caloric input that global children receive and study the discrepancies.

11th Grade Lesson Plan

Lesson Plan Title: Equality for All

Designers: Kathy Keffeler, Chelsea Edge, Colleen Parker, Deborah Bohn, Joe Underwood

Grade: 11

Time Frame: Two lessons of 50 minutes minutes

Subjects: Civics, Language Arts, Media, Global Affairs, Social Studies

Instructional Goal: Promote higher level thinking skills regarding the meaning of equality, cultural awareness, and personal responsibility to influence global equality. Create an individual action plan to create and foster equality and address inequalities.

Standards: UN Sustainable Development Goal Number 16: Peace, Justice and Strong Institutions

Understanding:

2: Ethical Orientation

 B: Commitment to basic equality of all people

Essential Question:

1. In what ways can advocating for equality on a local level lead to more global cultural awareness and citizenship?

Student Learning Objectives: Students will identify inequalities among citizens at either the local, state, national, or global level and take measurable action (letters, videos, fundraisers, research papers, presentations or community service) to address those inequalities while advocating for equality for all. Their actions/projects/assessments will highlight the importance of advocacy, equality, and cultural awareness.

Sequence of Activities:

 Step 1: Educated students on UN Sustainable Development Goals -- possible options:

- Small groups WebQuest what these are. Each group reports on two or three of the goals.
- Provide a hand out or direct students to UN website to read and summarize the UN Sustainable Development Goals. They can summarize in a one-page informative essay or via a two-minute PowerPoint presentation.
- Direct students to the UN Sustainable Development Goals website (http://www.un.org/sustainabledevelopment/sustainable-development-goals/), introduce the UN Sustainable Deelopment Goal concept, and review with focus on the UN Sustainable Development Goal #16: Peace, Justice, and Strong Institutions.
- Show a UN Sustainable Develpoment Goals video. Use a Jigsaw activity with six pairs each completing three goals and reporting what they learned to the class.

Next day -- Whole Class: Quick review of UN Sustainable Development Goals

Today we focus on Goal Number 16 "Ethical Orientation" /Commitment to Basic Equality of All People"

Step2: Identify Inequalities and Justices at Multiple Levels. Options:

- Use a white board for students to list instances of inequality or injustice on local, national, AND international levels
- Create a Padlet and each student post a visual image of inequality? (e.g., lights of earth from space? Gay citizens in jails? Poor school room vs. wealthy? Water in Flint, Michigan?)
- Students will work collaboratively in groups to conduct research on inequality in education or wealth or justice throughout several countries. Students will

be able to gather information from several credible sources to compare and contrast education standards in different countries.

- Bring focus to UN Sustainable Development Goal Number 16: Small groups brainstorm and report out instances of inequality at national, state and local levels with larger group.
- Students identify local, state, and national inequality issues with a search of newspapers online and record their findings to share to class.
- Students will work with groups to answer the following questions: Why do inequalities in your community matter? Why do inequalities in your country matter? Why do global inequalities matter? If a child in Syria does not receive an education, how might it affect you?

Step 3: Students Propose Solutions. Options:

- Have students write a one paragraph solution proposal.
- Students brainstorm possible solutions in small groups, and then share out verbally or via PowerPoint or Padlet.
- Students create a one-slide PowerPoint with visuals and a proposed solution.
- Small groups research/WebQuest organizations that are already working toward solutions. Who they are and what they do at national, state and local level. Students decide at what level they'd like to advocate: (e.g. Prezi/PowerPoint/Posters/Flyers/Video Share with class).
- Students will vote to choose one or two injustices to address and decide their own steps to advocate.

Step 4: Assessment

- Students will take their research and write a script for an educational video report of approximately two minutes. This script will then be produced and edited into a video package that can be used as either a portion of content for the school's television newscast and/or be used as a stand-alone message to be posted on a social media platform such as YouTube, Twitter, Facebook, Instagram, or another appropriate site. The two-minute video will be assessed for content, alignment with UN Sustainable Development Goal Number 16, and the creative process of proper editing with visuals, voice-over, and (if applicable) appropriate music and sound.
- Write a three-page research paper explaining the UN Sustaible Development Goals, describing one injustice, tracing its history in the area, nation, or world, providing examples of this inequality, and identifying possible solutions. Use a minimum of five sources. MLA format. Send this paper to the elected official with the power to enact the call to action/solution suggested in the paper.
- Small groups will create a project to support their chosen issue and determine what steps are needed to advocate and change the inequality with a rubric to grade peers projects. Extension: Study Collaborative Groups for AVID Tutorial or study a question which arose which no group can answer.
- Small groups create a mini campaign to encourage others to support/join their chosen researched cause. Pace posters, videos, flyer, presentations across the district and in the community library for a designated "UN Human Rights Day" to showcase student findings and solutions.
- Create a persuasive speech on the issue and deliver it to the student body, the school board or the city council. The speech must contain a hook, several statistics from reliable sources, and a call to action.
- Students develop a formal letter to an elected representative advocating for a plan of action to address inequality in their community. The letter must contain statistics and facts from reliable sources to prove the inequality exists. It must contain

a reasonable call to action, for example a change to a law or funding.

- Big Idea Project: Student groups will receive an envelope with a mystery amount of money. Their job will be to come up with a plan to address a local inequality based on the amount of money their group receives. The plan must include where the money is spent, what people it helps, and the long-term effects of the plan/action. The plan must include graphics, a write up, and a presentation to the class. Students are encouraged to think big and "out of the box." See Resources for ideas.
- Investigate and join an existing charity or organization that works to address the issue/cause/charity, e.g., Amnesty International, UNICEF, etc. Donate X number of hours or raise money for this group.
- Create a local club for awareness and support of issue/cause/charity. Students must get administrative approval for the club, recruit members, create marketing materials, and hold at least four meetings a semester with teacher oversight.

Resources:

- UN Sustainable Development Goals website: http://www.un.org/sustainabledevelopment/sustainable-development-goals/)
- Sample MLA research paper with hook, statistics, and call to action https://depts.washington.edu/owrc/Handouts/Hacker-Sample%20MLA%20Formatted%20Paper.pdf
- Template letter to an elected offical: https://www.sps186.org/downloads/basic/642616/LettertoCongress.pdf
- Persuasive speech template: https://www.write-out-loud.com/support-files/persusasive-speech-outline.pdf
- Sample video addressing inequities in water, wealth, food, and health in Nicaragua

http://www.miamiseniorhigh.org/apps/video/watch.jsp?v=
10030732
- Steps to create an awareness campaign
  https://psacorp.com/main/default/t-creating-a-successful-
  awareness-campaign.aspx
    - Exisiting charities to join or assist with raising
      money:
      ○ https://worldhelp.net/donate-
        goats/?utm_source=Google&utm_medium=SEM&u
        tm_campaign=GoatsNew_2017_986&gclid=Cj0KCQ
        jwl7nYBRCwARIsAL7O7dFRoI2QMuv_XKnRdtf07
        GTYe-uX4gDJaD-
        mQpi3ArBi6Yi2YXHKFlYaAtBfEALw_wcB
      ○ https://www.malarianomore.org/
      ○ https://www.unicef.org/

- Big "out of the box" ideas to address inequalities

    ○ https://cleantheworldfoundation.org/mobile-
      hygiene-unit/
    ○ https://www.youtube.com/watch?v=jT-
      nhBVxrqA#action=share
    ○ https://www.dawn.com/news/694200

12th Grade Lesson Plan

Lesson Plan Title: Capstone Project AKA Students Are Teachers, Too!

Designer: Noah Zeichner, Vasiliki Dardeshi, and Kimberley Gilles

Summary and Rationale:

12th grade students will have the opportunity to adapt what they are learning to teach younger students and/or peers a lesson that addresses one or more of the UN Sustainable Development Goals.

The plan will assist with raising student awareness about meaningful issues facing our global community and require seniors to demonstrate essential 21st century skills (being a self-directed learner, working as a collaborative team member, being an effective communicator, being a global citizen, and demonstrating information and technological literacy).

Grade: 12

Time Frame: 45-60 minutes for 12th grade student-led lesson. The number and length of preceding lessons depends on subject area and curricular context.

Subjects: Social Studies, Language Arts, Science, Math, Art, World Languages...,

Instructional Goals:

1. Intercultural competency
    a. Interpersonal Skills
        i.   Demonstrate empathy toward other people from different cultural origins
        ii. Demonstrate courtesy and norms of interaction appropriate to various cultural settings
    b. Intrapersonal Skills
        i.   Curiosity about global affairs and world cultures
        ii. An understanding and appreciation of cultural variation in basic norms of interaction, the ability to be courteous, and the ability to find and learn about norms appropriate in specific settings and types of interaction

104

2. Ethical Orientation
   a. Ability to interact with people from diverse cultural backgrounds while demonstrating humility, respect, reciprocity, and integrity
3. Work Ethic and Habits of Mind
   a. Demonstrate innovation and creativity in contributing to formulating solutions to global challenges and to seizing global opportunities; seek and identify the best global practices; and transfer them across geographic, disciplinary and professional contexts.
   b. Carry out research projects independently.
   c. Present results of independent research orally, in writing, and using media.
      i. See Student Lesson Plan Template at the end of this project description

UN Sustainable Development Goalss: (Potentially all depending on student projects).

All UN Sustainable Development Goals

Understanding: Students will demonstrate understanding of transnational issues by researching and presenting UN Sustainable Development Gs.

Essential questions:

1. What issues in today's world do you see as global issues?
2. Why and how do these issues impact people, societies, and the world?

Student Learning Objectives:

1. Become familiar with and explain the UN Sustaiable Development Goals.
2. Conduct research and analyze the current transnational issues.
3. Present research to an audience of younger students, thereby activating understanding of and empathy for a vulnerable audience.
4. Alternatively, present the lesson to a peer audience, thereby activating a sense of the broad spectrum of backgrounds that a group of peers

encompasses. Students learn to see their classmates differently and more clearly, a necessary precursor for authentic empathy.

5. Utilize multiple modes of communication effectively and enthusiastically.

Assessment:

- High school students complete a self-evaluation of their teaching.
- Teacher observes group's interactions with students looking for evidence of:
  - Clear communication of ideas
  - Shared responsibility of leadership
  - Benchmark assignments

Research Benchmarks

1. Research how the problems addressed by the UN's Sustainable Development Goals affect the world, even the student's community.
2. Identify the one Sustainable Goal that your country or issue group will focus on and the specific problem that relates to this goal.
3. Explain the root causes of this problem in your community, your nation or in an assigned country.
4. Present evidence, reasons, and/or research that makes it clear to the audience that this problem should be a top priority.
5. Explain what is already being done to address the problem, the progress made to date, and the challenges that might prevent your country, organization, or community from achieving its goals.

Sequence of Activities: List the sequence of events for this lesson. Include an opener (motivator), core events of the lesson and a conclusion. Indicate how students should be grouped and the question or provocation that will guide their work in each event.

Prior Learning:

- Teacher or student-led instructional unit that incorporates one or more of the UN Sustainable Development Goals. (The instructional unit may be non-fiction reading which include research, ancillary materials, and biographies.)
- Student-driven research project investigating one or more of the UN Sustainable Development Goals.

○ Have students get into groups -- teacher or student selected -- and research an UN Sustainable Development Goal that most motivates them.

Teacher Preparation:

- Set up a partnership with another teacher if working with a younger group or with another section of your course in your school. Work with younger grade levels (if there is no elementary or middle school nearby, work with younger grades in your own school).

- If there is resistance in your school to "interrupting" other classes, the teacher may choose to make the research projects a strand in the class curriculum that recurs throughout the year.

- When working with the partner teacher, identify links between curricula. For example, if a 4th grade class is learning about ecosystems in science, the high school teacher can highlight ways for the high school students to connect their lesson plans to that content.

- Set up the logistics of the classroom visit. This may involve walking or taking the bus. If you set up a series of three visits in a semester, the younger students could visit the high school for the final visit. Take care of any administrative requirements for field trips (permission forms, etc.). Videoconferencing is an alternative option as well. The high school students can be in groups of four or five and they can work with small groups of younger students.

Preparation for the Classroom Visit:

1. Have students think about the most engaging lesson that they have experienced in school (at any age). Ask them to reflect on what made that lesson interesting and exciting? Could they relate it to their lives? Were they creating something (rather than just listening to a teacher lecture)?

2. Provide students with a lesson plan template and provide a brief overview of the lesson-development process.

3. Now, have them enter the information they have researched into the lesson plan template -- remembering the most interesting and exciting lessons they considered in question number 1, shown above! They can adapt lessons that they did in class for a younger audience.

4. Collect and review the lessons plan and provide feedback. Encourage the students to incorporate hands-on activities.
5. Have students collect any materials they need to teach the lesson.
6. If visual aids are going to be included, provide time and art materials. A technological tool may include- PowerPoint, Prezi, Movie Maker, Kahoot, etc.
7. Provide time in class for students to practice giving the lesson. Ask them to revise the lesson if they notice any "holes." Have students rehearse giving directions to the younger students or peers. Role play potential challenges (younger students not listening, etc.).

Day of Classroom Visit or Presentation:

1. Deliver a lesson that informs and engages the audience around your Global Sustainable Goal.
2. Start with a brief overview of the Global Sustainable Goal and its objectives.
3. The lesson should be interactive, with hand-on learning activities (art, literature, music, math, science). The lesson should begin with a hook or ice-breaker. The lesson should reference any previous readings and/or introductory classroom instruction. The lesson should have a clear conclusion where student learning can be formatively assessed.
4. If the high school students teach their lessons to younger students in small groups, gather the whole class at the end of the visit and have the high school students ask the younger students to reflect on what they learned. The teacher can select one or two high school students to call on the younger students.
5. If the high school students teach to their peers, the student-teachers will assign homework that they design and will write a reflection on what they learned, and art of teaching.

Possible extensions:

1. Discuss in small groups (either within the 12th grade class or with the 12th grade presentation team and partner classroom) action steps to take related to the learning that happened. Create a "Call to Action." For example, perhaps the learning was related to hunger, or perhaps the students do an empty bowls fundraiser in order to help a family buy animals through Heifer International.

Digital resources for students:

- Research The Global Goals for Sustainable Development: http://www.undp.org/content/undp/en/home/sustainable-development-goals.html
- Food Security Council: http://foodsecuritycluster.net/
- CIA World Factbook: https://www.cia.gov/library/publications/the-world-factbook/
- UNDP Support to the Implementation of the UN Sustainable Development Goals: http://www.undp.org/content/undp/en/home/librarypage/sustainable-development-goals/undp-support-to-the-implementation-of-the-2030-agenda/
- Library databases: Students should be encouraged to find peer reviewed research-based articles.
- Print Materials:
  - The UN Sustainable Development Goals
  - Atlas of Sustainable Development Goals 2017: From World Development Indicators (World Bank Atlas) by World Bank

Resources for teachers: List print or online resources that can help teachers prepare the lesson.

- School district's Online Library Catalog
- BBC Country Profiles
- Student Lesson Planning Templates, pages 6 through 10
- Proposed Rubrics for grading the entire lesson presentation, pages 11 through 14

Lesson Plan Templates, Rubrics, and Global Resources

Materials: <u>Fill out this section as you complete each of the lesson plan segments.</u>

Examples: computer, scissors, glue, tape, construction paper, index cards, markers

Review of information: Pre-Learning – preparations for the activity/analysis

Purpose: To review the information that the elementary class has covered, making the connection.

Or, to review the readings or information that peers have provided prior to the presentation.

- Estimated time required to teach: _____
- Activities and Interaction/Discussion Opportunities:
- Interaction with the ideas:

Purpose: To interact with the material in a way that activates prior experience and/or empathy. The interactions give the audience an opportunity to personalize the information with an experience. Discussion will result.

- Ex: Human Graph/Take a Stand/Simulation/Videos
- Estimated time required to teach: _____
- Activities and Interaction/Discussion Opportunities:

Conclusion:

- Purpose: To consider next steps (activism?) or to engage in reflection
- Estimated time required to teach: _____
- Other Possible Activities and Interaction/Discussion Opportunities:

Assign Homelearning: Assign ONLY if the student teachers and the classroom teachers determine homelearning is logical or necessary

- Write it on the board!
- Have it written and printed for distribution
- Estimated time required to explain the assignment:_____

- Answer any questions. Clarify any last details.
- Instructions for the homelearning <u>MUST include</u> the following reminders:
  - Format? (Picture? Bumper sticker? Brief essay? MLA? Design a temporary tattoo?)
  - Due date:

Alternate Lesson Plan Template

LESSON PLAN

Personal Leadership Goals: Write two specific ways that you're going to grow your leadership skills:

| |
| |
| |

Objectives of Lesson (What key lesson(s) will the students learn?):

1.
2.
3.

Detailed description of the icebreaker you plan on doing with the students:

| |
| |

Activity:

- ✓ Indicate number of minutes for each activity.

- ✓ Be very clear about including the lesson, questions/discussion, and your assessment of student learning.

- ✓ Explain exactly how you will carry out each activity - include details of what each of the teachers are doing (by name) and what the students are doing during each activity.

Activity/time	Exactly what teachers will do (include names)	Exactly what you want students to do
Lesson segment/ amount of time		
Activity/ Time	Exactly what teachers will do (include names)	Exactly what you want students to do

Lesson segment/ amount of time		

Materials and Preparation:

✓ Create a to-do list below of all of the materials and supplies needed and preparation that will need to be done before the field trip on Thursday. We will have most of class tomorrow (Tuesday). Make sure to note who on the team will do it. Make sure you check with Mr. Fischburg to see if we or Roxhill has any materials you will need.

A Sample Rubric for Evaluating Both Preparation and Presentation of a Topic

Name/s: _____ Date: _____

Topic: _____

Rubric: Presentation of Articles and Facilitation of Discussion

1.   Quality of the articles: the anchor article, the biography (BOTH are required!), and any ancillary materials you want printed for the class reader and presentation. (Consider the credibility of the publishing source, the credentials of the author, the clarity and strength of the writing, and the level of interest it may evoke in your students.) You are expected to present a minimum of one complete article or a substantial excerpt of an article from a peer reviewed (academic) journal AND the biography of a person directly affected by the issue under consideration. Additional sources may complement your academic piece. If you take a different approach, contact your teacher BEFORE the due date for your articles. Maximum: 30 pages

20 points   _____

2.   All deadlines met for submission, approval, copying, distribution, preparation of discussion questions/prompts and set up of materials.

   a.   Submission deadline: ONE WEEK before your Thursday scheduled presentation. (5 points)

   b.   Article approval deadline: The Friday before your presentation.   (5 points)

   c.   Copying deadline: The Monday before your presentation you will submit your articles for copying by LUNCH. (5 points)

   d.   Distribution deadline: The Tuesday before your presentation. (YOU must watch the school calendar and know when we are not in school on a Friday or a Monday. If that occurs, you are responsible for meeting all the deadlines early so that your classmates have time to read your WONDERFUL selections!) (5 points)

20 points   _____

117

3.   Submission of a written LESSON PLAN: The Monday before your presentation date you are expected meet with your teacher.

Your LESSON PLAN must include:

     a.   Preparation of written questions/prompts based upon the reading you assigned;   (4 points)

     b.   Activities for participation; (4 points)

     c.   Classroom technology required, as needed (4 points)

     d.   Additional materials you intend to use (art supplies, activity cards, scenarios, etc.), as needed; (4 points)

     e.   Proposed home learning assignment   (4 points)

20 points   _____

4.   The day of your presentation, the discussion and activities reflect preparation/rehearsal, creativity, and commitment to the ideas under consideration. Every member of the presentation is expected to interact with your classmates as they rise to meet the academic opportunities you provide.

20 points   _____

5.   Provide a prompt so that your classmates may write a reflection on the day's discussion or activity. Your prompt will be assigned as home learning. The reflections may be shared in a public reading at the beginning of class the next day or may be graded by your teacher. Occasionally, if the activity/assignment is thought-provoking, Ms. Gilles may authorize a different form of response. (See Lesson Plan Template for requirements.)

10 points   _____

TOTAL POINTS POSSIBLE: 90 points

TOTAL EARNED: _____

Additional Comments:

Alternate Rubric:

	Level 2	Level 3	Level 4
	EMERGING	COMPETENT	EXEMPLARY
1. Prepara-tion	No visuals or visuals with little forethought. High School leaders not confident in their teaching. Little evidence of preparation.	Visuals are used. High School leaders are somewhat confident in their teaching. Some evidence of preparation.	Visuals are educational and creative. High School leaders confident in their teaching. Clear evidence of preparation.
2. Content	Content has several errors and is incomplete. Unable to answer questions.	Content is somewhat complete. Some ease with answering questions.	Content is complete and accurate. Able to answer questions with explanation and elaboration.
3. Partici-pation	Some group members rely on others to complete tasks.	Some participation by all group members, content and questions answered by a few.	All members participate fully, actively; know content, answer questions and present material.

4. Presentation	Choppy and confusing lesson, difficult to follow, transitions abrupt. Encouragement is sparse. Directions to students are unclear.	Somewhat organized ideas not presented coherently, transitions not smooth. Encouragement is used somewhat. Directions to students are clear at times.	Extremely well organized, lesson follows a logical format, presentation flows smoothly. Encouragement is used appropriately and frequently. Directions to students are clear.
5. Voice	Most voices cannot be heard by all, most are unsteady, unclear, without inflection. Little or no eye contact with audience. Volume level is inappropriate for the classroom space.	Some voices can be heard, most voices are clear, tones are somewhat appropriate. Some members maintain eye contact with audience. Volume level is mostly appropriate for the classroom space.	All voices are loud, clear, with a friendly tone, appropriate inflection and steady. Eye contact is maintained with audience. Volume level is appropriate for the classroom space.
6. Question-ing Techniques	No open-ended questions are incorporated into lesson.	One or two questions are incorporated into the lesson. At least one question is	Several questions are incorporated into the lesson. Questions are open-ended,

		open-ended, connected to content and promotes discussion.	connected to content, promote discussion, and draw in audience.
7. Assessment	No assessment of student learning.	Some assessment of student learning, but results are unclear.	Clear evidence collected that shows how much students learned.
Comments			Total Score

Sample Global Lesson Plan Rubric
Monica Washington

Lesson Component	Traveling Good →	Gaining Speed Better →	Gone Global Great!
Summary and Essential Questions	Lesson summary is clear. Lesson contains 2-4 essential questions to help guide and frame the lesson.	Lesson summary is clear. Lesson contains 2-4 essential questions to help guide and frame the lesson. Questions and big ideas and understandings are aligned.	Lesson summary is clear. Lesson contains 2-4 essential questions to help guide and frame the lesson. Questions and big ideas/understandings are aligned and stimulate inquiry, discussion, and critical thinking about global issues.
Objectives and Standards	Objectives are specific. Objectives are appropriate for the lesson's specified grade level.	Objectives are specific and measurable. Objectives are appropriate for the lesson's specified grade level. Language in written objectives point to observable student actions such as "write" or "draw."	Objectives are specific and measurable. Objectives are appropriate for the lesson's specified grade level. Language in written objectives point to observable student actions such as "write" or "draw." Objectives are connected to criteria that guide teachers in the assessment of the objective.
Lesson Activities	Lesson activities are divided into clear sections that include motivating activities, core learning activities, and	Lesson activities are divided into clear sections that include motivating activities, core learning activities, and concluding activities. Lesson	Lesson activities are divided into clear sections that include motivating activities, core learning activities, and concluding activities. Lesson clearly describes student actions and grouping during the activities.

		clearly describes student actions and grouping during the activities.	Learning activities are aligned to global competencies.
	concluding activities.		
Assessment	A specific, grade-appropriate assessment has been designed that allows the teacher to determine whether students have met the objectives of the lesson.	A specific, grade-appropriate assessment has been designed that allows the teacher to determine whether students have met the objectives of the lesson. Assessment tools may include rubrics, tests, quizzes. Informal checks for understanding are included.	A specific, grade-appropriate assessment has been designed that allows the teacher to determine whether students have met the objectives of the lesson. The assessment aligns closely with lesson objectives and essential questions. Assessment tools may include rubrics, tests, quizzes. Informal checks for understanding are included.
Resources	Resources are included that help the teacher with planning and implementation of the lesson.	A variety of print and online resources is included to help the teacher with planning and implementation of the lesson. Resources support students in completing lesson activities.	A variety of print and online resources is included to help with planning, implementation, and integration of global objectives. Resources support students in completing lesson activities.

Global Learning Resources

Lesson Plans

International & Global Issues

Asia Society Center for Global Education
(http://asiasociety.org/education/lesson-plans)

Learn about Asia and the world through Asia Society's free lesson plans. See their International Studies Schools initiative for more information.
(http://asiasociety.org/international-studies-schools-network)

Global Oneness Project (https://www.globalonenessproject.org/lesson-plans)

The Global Oneness Project offers free multicultural stories and accompanying lesson plans for high school and college classrooms.

The World's Largest Lesson
(http://worldslargestlesson.globalgoals.org/#the-goals)

The World's Largest Lesson is a movement to teach young people about the Sustainable Development Goals and encourage them to become the generation that changes the world.

Council on Foreign Relations
(http://www.cfr.org/publication/interactives.html)

UN Cyber School Bus (http://www.unausa.org/global-classrooms-model-un/how-to-participate/model-un-preparation/research/cyberschoolbus)

Edutopia (https://www.edutopia.org/stw-global-competence-resources#graph1)

Frontline World (http://www.pbs.org/frontlineworld/educators/)

Global Dimension (https://globaldimension.org.uk/)

One World Education (https://www.oneworldeducation.org/one-world-program-curriculum)

PBS Learning Media (http://www.pbslearningmedia.org/collection/global-learning-and-awareness/?topic_id=919&utm_source=FW&utm_medium=Image&utm_campaign=Homepage)

Peace Corps World Wise Schools
(https://www.peacecorps.gov/educators/resources/)

Project Explorer (http://projectexplorer.org/ed/subjectsearch.php)

ReligionLesson.com (http://www.religionlesson.com/lesson-plans.html)

Teach UNICEF (http://teachunicef.org/)

Other Lesson Plans & Teaching Resources

Arts & Film

Kennedy Center's ArtsEdge (http://artsedge.kennedy-center.org/educators.aspx)

Journeys in Film (http://www.journeysinfilm.org/for-educators/the-store/)

Wide Angle Films (PBS) (http://www.pbs.org/wnet/wideangle/for-educators/lesson-plans/5668/)

STEM

Facing the Future (https://www.facingthefuture.org/)

Global Math Stories (http://www.globalmathstories.org/)

Various

Curriculum21 (http://www.curriculum21.com/clearinghouse/)

Curriki
(http://www.curriki.org/xwiki/bin/view/Coll_Group_TheNEAFoundationsPearsonFoundationGlobalLearningFellows/LessonscreatedbyGlobalLearningFellows)

Facing History & Ourselves (https://www.facinghistory.org/educator-resources)

Girls Thinking Global (http://girlsthinkingglobal.org/gtg-collaborative-visualization-tool/)

Global Campaign for Education
(http://campaignforeducationusa.org/pages/educational-curriculum)

Google World Wonders Project

US Institute of Peace (https://www.usip.org/public-education/educators)

Connecting Classrooms

Global Youth Debates (http://www.globalyouthdebates.com/)

 This Flat Connections global project provides a unique global collaborative experience for joining diverse cultures in authentic debate to foster global competence, international mindedness and action. It is suitable for all learning environments and is designed for students of age 10-18.

iCollaboratory (http://www.icollaboratory.org/)

The iCollaboratory provides K-12 teachers timely professional development, project consulting, training, technical advice, and Web-based resources and services to practice 21st century learning.

iEARN (http://www.iearn.org/)

iEARN (International Education and Resource Network) is the world's largest non-profit global network that enables teachers and youth to use the internet and other technologies to collaborate on projects that enhance learning and make a difference in the world.

Know My World (http://knowmyworld.org/)

Know My World hosts a variety of cross-cultural exchanges using various forms of digital technology and project based learning.

Rock Our World (http://rockourworld.org/)

Rock Our World connects students and teachers to collaborate in composing original music, making movies, and meeting each other in live video chats. Using Apple's GarageBand, each country creates a 30-second drumbeat.

World We Want (http://www.worldwewant2015.org/)

The World We Want web platform is a joint initiative between the United Nations and Civil Society. The World We Want is a growing movement of people all over the world contributing their vision towards an overall plan to build a just and sustainable world free from poverty.

Professional Development Programs and Resources

IREX: Teachers for Global Classrooms
(https://www.irex.org/project/teachers-global-classrooms-program-tgc)

Earthwatch Institute Teacher Fellowships
(http://earthwatch.org/education/teacher-fellowships)

EF Education First (https://www.ef.edu/)

InterAmerican Teacher Education Network (ITEN)
(http://oas.org/en/iten/professional.asp)

National Geographic Grovesnor Teacher Fellowship
(https://www.nationalgeographic.org/education/programs/grosvenor-teacher-fellows/)

State Department Bureau of Educational and Cultural Affairs Programs
(Multiple) (https://eca.state.gov/programs-initiatives)

Title VI Resource Centers
(https://www2.ed.gov/programs/iegpsnrc/index.html)

University of Minnesota Institute for Global Studies
(https://cla.umn.edu/global-studies/outreach-engagement/professional-development-educators)

Book Contributors

Fernando M. Reimers, Ed.D.
Ford Foundation Professor of the Practice of International Education
Director, International Education Policy, Harvard Graduate School of
Education

He is an expert in the field of Global Education, his research and teaching focus on understanding how to educate children and youth so they can thrive in the 21st century. He leads the Global Education Innovation Initiative, a research and practice collaborative in 15 countries, focused on supporting the transformation of public education to empower students to live well and contribute to their communities.

Recent books include *Teaching and Learning for the 21st Century, Preparing Teachers to Educate Whole Students: An International Comparative Study, Empowering Global Citizens, Empowering Students to Improve the World in Sixty Lessons. Version 1.0, Learning to Collaborate for the Global Common Good, Fifteen Letters on Education in Singapore, (Empowering All Students at Scale)*, and *One Student at a Time. Leading the Global Education Movement.*

He serves on the board of Massachusetts Board of Higher Education and in the board of directors of Facing History and Ourselves, World Teach, Teach for All, the Global Scholars Program at Bloomberg Philanthropies, Envoys, and other education organizations. In 2017 he received the Global Citizen Award from the Committee on Teaching about the United Nations for his work advancing global citizenship education. In 2015 he was appointed the C.J. Koh Visiting Professor of Education at the National Institute of Education in Singapore in recognition of his work in global education. He received an honorary doctorate from Emerson College for his work advancing human rights education. He is a fellow of the International Academy of Education and a member of the Council of Foreign Relations.

NEA Foundation Staff Contributors

Robert Adams Jr., Ph.D.
Senior Vice President of Programs
The NEA Foundation

Robert is the Senior Vice President for Programs at the NEA Foundation. He oversees programs for individual educators, including professional development opportunities, educator collaboration, and small grants to fund new courses, including the Global Learning Fellowship and Grants to Educators programs. He brings 17 years of philanthropic experience and 30 years of international experience to the Foundation. Robert's unique perspective on education and leadership comes from his previous work in Brazil, the Dominican Republic, Haiti, Mexico, Mozambique, Portugal, Spain, South Africa, and the United States. At the Foundation, Robert leverages his experience to help educators become leaders in the classroom and beyond.

Kristen Shannon
Program Manager
The NEA Foundation

Kristen works to strengthen students' global and cultural competencies by overseeing the NEA Foundation's global programs. She is the program manager of the Global Learning Fellowship - a year-long professional development program designed for American public school k-12 teachers to develop the knowledge and skills to integrate global competency into their daily classroom instruction to help prepare students for 21st century global citizenship.

An alumna of American University, she completed her BA in international studies with foci in international development, public administration, and policy. Kristen also studied community development at the University of KwaZulu-Natal in Durban, South Africa. She is passionate about seeking out ways to bridge the divide between local and international concerns through progressive approaches to education.

Before joining the Foundation, Kristen worked for a variety of State-Department accredited student and teacher exchange programs, including the Kennedy-Lugar Youth Exchange and Study (YES) program and the Future Leaders Exchange (FLEX) program.

Harriet Sanford
President & CEO
The NEA Foundation

Harriet Sanford is the President and CEO of the NEA Foundation, a position she has held since 2005. During her 12-year tenure with the Foundation, Sanford has transformed the depth and breadth of its programs and grant making by investing in educators to improve their instructional practice and unleash their own power, ideas and voices, so that communities, schools and students all benefit.

Sanford began her professional journey as a public school classroom teacher, which led to a senior executive career spanning more than 30 years with nonprofit and public organizations, including the Arts and Science Council in Charlotte, North Carolina, and the Fulton County Arts Council, in Georgia. Immediately prior to joining the NEA Foundation, Sanford served as the conceptual lead and manager of "South by South Africa: Crafting Cultural Understanding," a project that built economic links and cultural understanding between South Africa and U.S. partner cities. Her career is bound together by an unwavering commitment to strengthening community by building on the skills, talents and aspirations of each of its members.

Sanford holds a BA in education from New England College, a MPA from the University of Connecticut, and was awarded the degree of Doctor of Humane Letters from the University of Connecticut's Neag School of Education in 2015.

2018 Global Learning Fellow Contributors

Kimberly Amen
1st and 2nd Grade Gifted and Talented Educator
Cheyenne, WY

Kimberly has a BA in elementary education and an MPA from the University of Wyoming. She has experience both developing and implementing the two-year curriculum for her school's Gifted and Talented program. Kimberly also serves on her school's leadership team. She is the treasurer for the Wyoming Education Association and a trustee for the Wyoming Educator Benefit Trust. She also has experience working as a Head Start coordinator.

Debbie Anderson
Library Media Specialist
Hilo, HI

Debbie has over 10 years of teaching experience, spanning from various grade levels of the k-12 spectrum. She has a M.Ed. in special education from the University of Washington and a Master's of Library and Information Science from the University of Hawaii. She was previously awarded the Technology Educator Award from the Milken Foundation of Hawaii and is a member of Teacher Leader Initiative for Center for Teaching Quality. Debbie currently serves as an NEA Care Assessment Co-Chair and is the Hawaii State Teachers Association chapter president.

Heather Anderson
2nd Grade Educator
Des Moines, IA

Heather currently teaches 2nd grade and has experience as a lead kindergarten teacher. She has a BA in elementary education from Upper Iowa University and a MA in education from Viterbo University. Heather was awarded South Central Iowa's 2017 STEM Teacher Award and is a 2015 NEA Foundation Award for Teaching Excellence recipient. Heather was also a finalist for 2013 Iowa Teacher of the Year and for the 2013 Izaak Walton League Iowa Teacher of the Year. She currently serves on the Des Moines school board and is a member of the Iowa Outstanding Educators Advisory Council (DOE). She is affiliated with Des Moines Public School Foundation.

Terri Anderson
Special Education Educator
Gill, MA

Terri has experience teaching students from all grade levels across the k-12 and university-level spectrum. She has a BA in special education from Millersville University and a MA in education with a focus in learning disabilities from Northern Arizona University. Terri has experience as an education therapist and an adult basic education educator. She is currently a lead special education teacher and a grade-level leader. Terri represents special educators in her local union affiliate.

Jeremy Aten
Title 1 Reading Specialist
Weaverville, NC

Jeremy is an elementary school Title 1 Reading Specialist. He is National Board Certified and has over 20 years of classroom experience. He has a BS in elementary education from Mansfield University of Pennsylvania and a MA in reading education from Appalachian State University. Jeremy traveled to Japan as a 2006 recipient of the Japan Fulbright Memorial Scholarship, and to Greece and Turkey as a 2011 recipient of the Fulbright-Hayes Scholarship. Jeremy also has previous experience as a test assessor for Pearson.

Erin Austin
AP Art History Teacher
Fort Collins, CO

Erin currently teaches French and AP art history to high school students. She has experience teaching art at the elementary and middle school levels, as well as French at the middle school and high school levels.In addition to teaching, Erin has experience as an EF Global Education Ambassador. She is a 2005 recipient of the Hanson Scholarship for Educators and a 2007 recipient of the National Endowment for Humanities study abroad grant. In 2013, Erin was named Big Sister of the Year by the Twin Cities chapter of Big Brother Big Sister.She has a BA in French and art education from Gustavus Adolphus College and a MA in curriculum and instruction from University of St. Tomas.

Norman Ayagalria
English Language Arts and Yugtun Language Educator
Bethel, AK

Norman has a BA in English from the University of Alaska Fairbanks and.
He has experience teaching reading and writing in the native Alaskan Yup'ik
language to 3rd, 4th, 5th and 6th graders. Norman previously served as a
grant reviewer for the U.S. Department of Education Alaska Native
Education Equity (ANEP) program. He also former Bethel city council
member.

Anu Bajpai
STEM Educator
Windsor Mill, MD

Anuradha has a wide range of teaching experience in science content areas
such as biology and microbiology. She serves as a team leader, mentor, and
magnet program coordinator for her school. She has an MPhil Jiwaji
University and a MA in teaching from University of Gwalior in India.
Anuradha has received many grants, including the eco-classroom Costa Rica
Award from Northrup Grumman. She is a 2016 Naval Academy Summer
Academy participant and traveled to Indonesia that same year as a part of her
experience as an IREX Teachers for Global Classrooms Fellow.

Brett Bigham
Special Education Educator
Portland, OR

Brett is a special educator for Portland Public Schools. He has a BA in
communications from Oregon State University, as well as an MS in special
education from Portland State University. Brett was the 2014 Oregon State
Teacher of the Year, and is a 2015 NEA Foundation Award for Teaching
Excellence recipient. Brett w is also a former NEA LGBT Caucus National
Teacher Role Model Award recipient. He has experience as a functional living
skills transition program teacher for students with severe handicaps and
emotional disturbances. Inspired by wanting to bring the world to his
classroom, Brett has developed a series of ability guidebooks to help students
of varying abilities navigate the key global cultural sites.

Deborah Bohn
AP Literature and Honors English Educator
Thompson's Station, TN

Deborah teaches AP and honors English. She has experience teaching various levels of English and previously worked as a professional writer. She has written for many publications including Walt Disney, Nashville Parent Magazine, and Cincinnati Parent Magazine. Deborah also previously served as both a communications and public relation officer for the U.S. Navy.Deborah has a BA in English language and literature from the University of Virginia and a M.Ed. from Lipscomb University.

Monica Bryant
Career Preparation and SEL Educator
Las Vegas, NV

Monica is an elementary school counselor and teaches lessons on around concepts of academics, career, and social emotional learning. She has experience teaching kindergarten, 5th and 3rd grades. She has a BA in early childhood education from the University of Louisville and a M.Ed. in school counseling from the University of Louisville. She is a member of Zeta Phi Beta Sorority Incorporated. Monica is active as an executive board member and building representative for her local union affiliate.

Karyn Burgess
Special Education Educator
Manchester, NH

Karyn is a middle school special education teacher. She has a BA in education, with a focus in special education from Fitchburg State University. She also has experience both teaching and serving as an assessment administrator coordinator at Saint Paul American School in the Philippines.

Carah Casler
ESOL Educator
Pataskala, OH

Carah has more than 20 years of classroom experience. She is currently teaches 5th and 6th grade English Language Learners. She has a BA in history and German and a MA in second language acquisition with a specialization in Teaching English to Speakers of Other Languages (TESOL). Carah is a board member of Dresden Sister City International and previously served on the advisory board for the Eastland-Fairfield Vocational School Performing Arts Program

Donna Cuyler
Visual Arts Educator
Milwaukee, WI

Donna has been teaching high school art for over 20 years. She has a BFA with a certificate in teaching from University of Wisconsin - Whitewater and a MA in visual arts from Cardinal Stritch University. Donna is the recipient of many grants, including the Target Field Trip grant, the Potawatomi Grant, and the NEA Foundation Student Achievement Grant. Donna has participated in several professional development opportunities, including the National Endowment for the Humanities summer institute.

Betsy Dardeshi
Social Studies Educator
Doylestown, PA

Betsy teaches de-colonization and other social studies courses. She has taught at both the middle and high school level. She also has experience as a teacher instruction rater for the Posse Foundation's Measures of Effective Teaching (MET) project. Betsy has a BA in German literature and European studies, and a M.Ed. in education administration and supervision. She previously won the Morris County Educational Technology Training Center Lesson Plan Contest and was the second place nationwide winner of the 2016 University of Arizona Middle East Lesson Plan Competition.

Shayne Dove
Social Studies Educator
Cedar Springs, MI

Shayne has experience teaching social studies at the middle and high school level. He was involved in writing culture and ability inclusive curriculum for the Transatlantic Outreach Program and the Foreign Policy Institute. Shayne is a member of Cedar Springs Technology Committee and is a former participant in the of his school and district improvement team. He has a BA in education with a minor in History from Central Michigan University, and a M.Ed. in curriculum and instruction from the American College of Education.

Chelsea Edge
English Language Arts Educator
Portland, TX

Chelsea began her teaching career internationally with a Fulbright grant to teach in Germany as a participant on the Japan Exchange and Teaching (JET) Program. She currently teaches high school English and language arts. Chelsea was able to develop a partnership with her high school in Texas and the Takoma Ryukaku High School in Japan by connecting students through video and pen pal exchanges.

She has a BA in English from Southwestern University and a MA in international studies from the University of Wyoming. She also has post baccalaureate certifications in Secondary English, ESL and Special Education.

Andrea Eisenberger
Visual Arts Educator
Virginia Beach, VA

Andrea is a high school art teacher in Virginia Beach, VA. She has seven years of teaching experience. She obtained her BFA in studio art from Old Dominion University and her MAT in art education from the University of North Carolina at Charlotte. Andrea is passionate about building partnerships that are a benefit to both her local community and her students, as well as finding innovative ways to bring the world to her classroom.

Kelly Elder
Social Studies Educator
Helena, MT

Kelly currently teaches middle school social studies. He has experience teaching a plethora of classes including AP government, American democracy, American history, psychology, and economics. Kelly also has experience teaching at the secondary level through his involvement as a Montana Exchange Teacher for the Office of Public Instruction in Japan. Kelly is the 2017 Montana State Teacher of the Year and active member of the Ongoing Bargaining Committee for Helena Public Schools. He is also on the board for the National Board for Professional Teaching Standards. Kelly has a BA in economics from the University of Montana, Missoula and MA in political science from Montana State.

Sonia Galaviz
5th Grade Educator
Boise, ID

Sonia is a 5th grade elementary teacher. She has taught at the primary and intermediate grade level, in addition to teaching as an adjunct faculty for University of Phoenix and Boise State University. She is currently pursuing her doctorate degree from Boise State University and has a BA in elementary education and MA in curriculum and instruction, with an emphasis on bilingual education. She has received many honors, including being named as the 2009 Idaho Woman of the Year from the Idaho Business Review. In 2011, Sonia received the Excellence in Culturally Responsive Pedagogy from Teaching Tolerance. She is also a 2017 recipient of the NEA Foundation Award for Teaching Excellence. She serves on the state board for the Idaho Education Association and previously served as an outreach coordinator for the Idaho Commission on Hispanic Affairs.

Kimberley Gilles
English Educator
Danville, CA

Kimberley has experience teaching a variety of subjects at the middle and high school level, including English, art, and leadership. She currently teaches English at Monte Vista High School in California. Kimberley received her

BA in English from the University of California, and has a M.Ed. in curriculum and instruction with specialization in integration of the arts from Lesley University. She has receive many honors for her commitment to education, including the 2014 NEA Foundation Award for Teaching Excellence and the California Teachers Association Member Human Rights Award. Kimberley served as state representative for the California Teachers Association, and as a member of the California Teachers Association Women's Caucus. She has written several publications, including a piece on teaching the Laramie Project that was featured in the Rethinking Schools text *Sexism, Gender, and Sexuality.*

Emily Hatch
Music Educator
Daegu, South Korea

Emily has a BA in music and a MA in cross-cultural international education. As a general music and band teacher at Daegu American School in South Korea, she has developed a robust band program for middle school, teaching all musical levels of students (beginning, intermediate, and advanced) of grades 6-8 in one class and integrated music into the school culture. Emily received the Teaching Award from the Daegu American School for developing a music program that helped to both strengthen the parent-teacher connections and pilot the Model Cornerstone Assessments for the National Core Arts Standards.

Craig Hendrick
STEM Educator
Indianapolis, IN

Craig is currently a 6th grade math and science educator. He previously served as the Assistant Principal at Mary Bryan Elementary School. In this role, Craig helped plan and lead professional development and community activities within the school. Craig is a 2016-17 IREX Teachers for Global Classrooms Fellow and a 2005 Fulbright Memorial Fund Fellow. Earlier in his career, Craig taught for 8 weeks at Rangeview Primary School in Mitcham, Australia through a cultural immersion project as a student teacher. Craig earned his M.S.Ed from Indiana University Purdue University at Indianapolis. He holds a Gifted and Talented Professional Educator's License and Building Level Administrator Licenses.

Carly Imhoff
STEM Educator
Ashford, CT

Carly is a STEM elementary educator. She also has experience creating and implementing STEM programs for her school district, including piloting a 7th and 8th grade STEM cohort program to give students hands-on experience in STEM fields. To address a lack of services, Carly created and implemented a district-wide gifted and talented program. She has a BA in human ecology from the College of the Atlantic and an MSW with a focus in Community Organizing from the University of Connecticut.

Kathy Keffeler
Spanish & ESOL Educator
Douglass, SD

Kathy has experience as an English as a Second Language (ESOL) instructor, as well as a k-12 homebound instructor, translator and world language reader/scorer. Kathy has participated in numerous international professional development opportunities, including participating in the Toyota International Teacher Program to Costa Rica, Fulbright Educational Seminars, Uruguay Educator Exchange Program, and the American Council on Teaching Foreign Languages Scholarship to ECELA Spanish Immersion School in South America. She has a BS in education from the University of South Dakota and a MS in curriculum and instruction from Black Hills State University.

Angela Madsen
English Language Arts & Social Studies Educator
Omaha, NE

Angela currently works as a reading specialist and current events teacher. In 2015, Angela received the Nila Banton Smith Award for Outstanding Theory into Practice from the International Literacy Association. She was previously recognized as the Nebraska Middle School Teacher of the Year. Angela received her BS in Education and her MS in reading from the University of Nebraska.

Michelle McClaine
English Language Arts Educator
Kansas City, KS

Michelle earned her BGS in literature, language, and writing and has a MAT. She currently teaches English to high school students and serves as her school's drama club sponsor. Michelle also works for the Greater Kansas City Writing Project as a Teacher Consultant/Facilitator, where she designs and leads professional development around writing.

Sarah Merchlewitz
Special Education Educator
New York, NY

Sarah teaches 6th - 8th grade special education. She is TESOL certified and is the lead for her school's restorative justice program. Sarah received her BA in liberal arts from Sarah Lawrence College and her MS in special education from the City College of New York.

Michele Metzler
Social Studies Educator
Hampden, ME

Michele earned her BA in U.S. history from Bates College and her M.Ed. from University of Maine. Michele has taught a variety of social studies courses including U.S. history, world history, global perspectives, sociology, and economics. Michele serves as co-President of Education Association 22.

Julie Midkiff
Visual Arts Educator
Mount Hope, WV

Julie is a National Board Certified elementary art teacher. She has a BS in art education, as well as and BA in advertising/graphic design in studio art from Concord University. Julie also has a MA in special education from Marshall University, and is currently enrolled in a curriculum and instruction doctorate program. She was awarded the Global Rural Trust Fellowship in 2013, which enabled her to study the connection between European/Mediterranean Art and the Appalachian Arts and Crafts Tradition.

Michael Morasse
Special Education Educator
Whitinsville, MA

Michael is a 1st grade special education teacher. He has over 20 years of teaching experience and obtained his undergraduate and graduate degree from Wheelock College in Boston, MA. Michael received his certificate of advanced graduate study degree in special education administration from Bridgewater State University. He has participated in the development of social sciences and history curricula in his school and provides workshops and ongoing support for his district on working with students impacted by dyslexia.

Ikechukwu Onyema
STEM Educator
East Orange, NJ

Ikechukwu currently teaches 11th grade chemistry. He also has experience teaching 6th and 7th grade English. In 2016, he was accepted into the New Jersey Education Association named Bolivar Graham Apprentice Fellowship. Ikechukwu has a BA in English literature from Rutgers University, and an M.S.Ed from University of Pennsylvania.

David Ostheimer
1st Grade Educator
Bear, DE

David is a 1st grade educator with experience teaching 2nd grade. He also previously served as his school's technology coordinator. David is an actively participates as a Delaware Teachers Institute Fellows. Through his participation in the Delaware Teachers Institute, he has developed multiple unit plans including *Open Sesame! - Islamic Stories Along the Silk Road* and *Silly Coyote: Tricksters are for Kids! Trickster Stories from the American West.*

Alicia Pahl-Cornelius
STEM Educator
Virginia Beach, VA

Alicia teaches middle school STEM. Before entering the teaching profession, Alicia was a geologist. She is National Board Certified and received her BS in Geology from Michigan State University and MA in Teaching from University of Louisville.

Colleen Parker
Special Education Educator
Mendota Heights, MN

Colleen has a BA in deaf studies from California State University, as well as an MA in special education from University of St. Thomas. Colleen currently works as a high school case manager and has experience as an elementary teacher. She has licenses in Specific Learning Disabilities, Emotional Behavior Disorder and Autism Spectrum Disorders.

Gina Parker
Physical Education Educator
Berwyn, IL

Gina has been teaching elementary physical education for over 17 years. She has received many awards, such as the 2017 Eastern Illinois University Alumni Leadership & Service Award. She is also the 2015 Illinois Association for Health, Physical Education, Recreation and Dance (IAHPERD) Elementary PE Teacher of the Year. Gina is the President of the Illinois Association for Health, Physical Education, Recreation, and Dance (IAHPERD). She has a MS in physical education and a BS in physical education from Eastern Illinois University. She also has an MA in school leadership from Concordia University.

Allison Riddle
Elementary Mentor Supervisor
Farmington, UT

Allison has more than 30 years of experience of teaching. She is currently the Elementary Mentor Supervisor for Davis School District, where she leads the mentoring of over three hundred new elementary teachers. Allison is the 2014 Utah Teacher of the Year and currently represents Utah's teachers as a member of Governor Herbert's Education Excellence Commission. Allison is a member of the National Network of State Teachers of the Year (NNSTOY), and serves as the Communications Officer for the Utah State Teachers of the Year (UTSTOY) chapter.

Emily Robinson
English Language Arts Educator
Atlanta, GA

Emily currently teaches English/Language Arts at Druid Hills High School, an International Baccalaureate school of which she is also graduate. She received her BA in English and M.Ed. in English education from the University of Georgia.

Maria Hannah Rodgers
STEM Educator
Pelham, AL

Hannah is currently the English as a Second Language (ESL) lead teacher at Riverchase Middle School, where she also has experience teaching Earth science, theatre, English/Language Arts, and social studies. She received her MA in speech and theatre education from University of Alabama and her BA in Communication from University of St. Thomas. Earlier in her career, she taught English as a Foreign Language in Shingu, Japan.

Darein Spann
English Educator
Jackson, MS

Darein currently teaches English to high school students; he also has experience teaching at the middle school level. He previously served as President of Jackson Association of Educators and currently serves on the NEA Board of Directors. Darein received his BA in English from Belhaven University and his M.Ed. from Mississippi College. He is currently pursuing his Doctorate of Education Leadership from Mississippi College.

Nanette Saumier-Trax
Reading Educator/Interventionist
O'Fallon, MO

Nanette is a reading interventionist in the Fort Zumwalt School District. She has experience teaching 1st through 3rd grade and English as a First Language (EFL). Nanette also has experience as a reading curriculum coordinator and a Gifted and Talented teacher. She has a BA in English from University of Michigan and a MA in education from Lindenwood University. Nanette previously served as a Parent Links liaison and advocate, and is the founder and coordinator of the Midwest Family Camp for Families with Deaf and Hard of Hearing children.

Dr. Joe Underwood
Media Arts Educator
Miami, FL

Joe has been teaching television production and media arts at Miami High School for over 30 years. He has a BA in speech and theater, a MS in sport science, and a Ph.D. in educational leadership. Joe has received numerous honors, including being named a Top 50 Finalist for the Varkey Foundation Global Teacher Prize and winning the 2011 NEA Foundation Award for Teaching Excellence. Joe has participated in an array of professional development programs, including the Japan-Fulbright Memorial Foundation Teacher Program and the Smithsonian Institute Learning Fellowship at the National Portrait Gallery.

Christa Wallace
Gifted and Talented Educator
Tulsa, OK

Christa has over 20 years of experience teaching elementary school in the Tulsa Public School District. She is currently a Gifted and Talented Coordinator and has experience developing curriculum based on Oklahoma state standards, as well as National Gifted Standards. Christa received her BS in education from Oklahoma State University.

Laura West
5th Grade Educator
Hot Springs, AR

Laura currently teaches 5th grade humanities and serves as the Gifted and Talented Coordinator for in the Hot Springs School District. Laura is National Board Certified and has a MS in curriculum and instruction. She has received numerous awards throughout her teaching career in the Hot Springs School District, including the District's Teacher of the Year Award in 2015. Laura has also participated in numerous professional development programs, including the Humanitarian Law Institute with Red Cross International, the Goethe Transatlantic Outreach Program, Gilder Lehrman Summer Seminar at Duke University, and the Fulbright-Hays Seminar Abroad Program to Poland.

Bessie Wright
Elementary Educator
Orangeburg, SC

Bessie has extensive experience with the Orangeburg Consolidated School District as an elementary teacher. She serves as the Five Education Association president, building leader, and ESSA team leader. She also serves as an executive board member for the South Carolina Education Association. She received her M.Ed., as well as her BA from South Carolina State University.

Noah Zeichner
Social Studies & Spanish Language Educator
Seattle, WA

Noah is a National Board Certified educator who has been teaching for over 15 years. He currently teaches high school social studies and Spanish. He has a BA history and Spanish from University of Wisconsin - Madison and his M.Ed. in teaching from University of Washington. Noah has received numerous awards, including the 2013 World Affairs Council World Educator Award, and the 2011 Philip B. Swain Excellence in Education Award. In 2015, Noah was previously named as a Top 50 Finalist for the Varkey Foundation Global Teacher Prize.

Global Learning Fellow Alumni Book Contributors

Jessica Anderson
Instructional Coach
Anaconda, MT
NEA Foundation Global Learning Fellow, Class of 2017

Jessica Anderson, the 2016 Montana Teacher of the Year, is a high school science teacher. Over nine years of teaching, her classroom approach evolved from traditional to a self-paced, blended-gamified environment. In 2014, she was chosen nationally as one of eleven BetterLesson Blended Master Teachers. She has also been recognized as a PBS Lead Digital Innovator (top 30), a state finalist for the 2015 Presidential Award for Excellence in Math and Science Teaching, and has received the Gold Star Award for Excellence in Teaching. Jessica also co-founded and facilitates #MTedchat, a participant-driven education chat on Twitter, In the summer of 2016, Jessica joined the team at BetterLesson as a Blended Learning Instructional Coach.

Anna Baldwin
High School English Educator
Arlee, MT
NEA Foundation Global Learning Fellow, Class of 2015

Anna Baldwin is a high school English teacher at Arlee High School and has been teaching on the Flathead Indian Reservation for the past 17 years. She designed and teaches Native American studies for the Montana Digital

Academy and taught English methods courses at the University of Montana for four years as an adjunct assistant professor.

She was selected as a 2016 Classroom Teaching Ambassador Fellow with the U.S. Department of Education. Baldwin is the recipient of several awards, including the Horace Mann Excellence in Teaching Award, Montana Association of Teachers of English Language Arts Distinguished Educator Award, and the Award for Excellence in Culturally Responsive Teaching from Teaching Tolerance.

She was the 2014 Montana Teacher of the Year.

Jeanne DelColle
Instructional Development & Strategic Partnerships Specialist
Absecon, NJ
NEA Foundation Global Learning Fellow, Class of 2013

Jeanne DelColle has been an educator for 20 years, 16 of which she taught high school social studies. An award winning teacher, she was named 2010 NJ Council for the Humanities Teacher of the Year, 2012 NJ History Teacher of the Year, and 2012 NJ State Teacher of the Year. Serving at the request of the Commissioner, Jeanne spent a year serving in a policy role at the NJ Department of Education as Educator Outreach Coordinator and worked to get information out and teacher voice in. While working at the NJDOE, she created and produced a monthly newsletter called The Bridge and established the New Jersey Teacher Advisory Panel, a group of 90 educators that met on a regional level to discuss education policy once a month with directors from various NJDOE divisions. Her interest in policy led her to be named a 2013 National Hope Street Group Fellow. In 2013, Jeanne was also named an NEA Foundation Global Fellow and examined the education system in Brazil. She is completing her doctorate in leadership, policy, and change in education and currently serves on the leadership team at Stockton University's School of Education as the Strategic Partnerships Specialist. There Jeanne works with students and the University's P-12 school partners to strengthen clinical education.

Mary Eldredge-Sandbo
High School Science Educator
Des Lacs, ND
NEA Foundation Global Learning Fellow, Class of 2012

Mary Eldredge-Sandbo has been teaching Des Lacs-Burlington High School in Des Lacs, North Dakota for over 30 years. She teaches biology and anatomy. Mary is a National Board Certified Teacher and the 2010 ND State Teacher of the Year. She participated in the NEA Foundation Global Learning Fellowship trip to China in 2012. She is currently working toward her doctorate in teacher leadership through Walden University. Mary lives in Des Laces with her husband and two dogs.

Luke Merchlewitz
Second Grade Educator
Winona, MN
NEA Foundation Global Learning Fellow, Class of 2011

Luke Merchlewitz received his BA in elementary education from the University of Minnesota, Minneapolis in 1983, and completed his education with a M.Ed. from Winona State University in 2001. He currently teaches second grade at Washington-Kosciusko Elementary School in Winona. An award winning teacher, Merchlewitz's accolades include: 2009 Winona Teacher of the Year, Minnesota Teacher of the Year Top 10 Finalist, and 2010 Minnesota Teacher of Excellence. He was also named a 2010 Top 10 Finalist for the NEA Foundation Teacher of Excellence in Washington D.C.; a 2011 NEA Foundation Global Learning Fellow; and an NEA Foundation Senior Global Learning Fellow, 2012 to present. In 2014 he was the Winona Area Public School's Foundation "Dare to Dream" recipient. He presented at the EF Global Leaders' Summit in Davos, Switzerland, in 2015 and the Maverick Teacher Global Summit in Kuppam, India, in 2016. A past Winona State University adjunct faculty member, a Teach 21 participant and speaker, he currently serves as the WAPS liaison member on the Education Village Task Force.

Peter Mili
Former Secondary Mathematics Educator
Cambridge, MA
NEA Foundation Global Learning Fellow, Class of 2013

Peter Mili is a former secondary school mathematics teacher, serving as an educator for more than 35 years in Cambridge, MA. He remains engaged in education pursuing his interest including effective use of educational technology, curriculum development, professional development, global competence, teaching, and supporting emerging educators to advance teaching and learning. Currently he serves as a Virtual Coach for the NEA's Early Career Learning Labs, a collaborator and presenter on mathematics learning resources for WhatifMath, and a member of the NEA's Common Core Working Group. Peter earned National Board Teacher Certification in 2000, was awarded a Mathematics Teacher/Scholar Fellowship by Focus on Math at Boston University in 2012, and was recognized as a Teacher of Excellence by the NEA Foundation and as a Global Learning Fellow in 2013.

Joan Soble
Former High School English Educator
Cambridge, MA
NEA Foundation Global Learning Fellow, Class of 2012

Joan Soble is a career educator and aspiring writer who consults in and beyond the United States with schools and organizations seeking to foster engaged student and teacher learning as well as student achievement. After more than thirty-four years as a school-based educator, Joan retired in 2014 from Cambridge Rindge and Latin School (CRLS) in Cambridge, MA, where she taught English language arts and supported the faculty's professional learning. Joan's twenty-four-year association with Project Zero (PZ) at the Harvard Graduate School of Education began when she was a research-teacher with the Teaching for Understanding Project and continued with her participation in the Making Learning Visible Project. Currently, in association with PZ's Interdisciplinary & Global Studies Project.

Joan mentors and provides professional development to participants in the Globalizing the Classroom Fellowship, an initiative co-sponsored by Harvard's global studies research centers. Joan sometimes writes about education in her blog, "So Already: A Blog about Moving Forward and Staying Connected" (soalready.blogspot.com).

Monica Washington
Instructional Coach
Texarkana, TX
NEA Foundation Global Learning Fellow, Class of 2015

Monica Washington is an instructional coach for BetterLesson. Previously, she taught English III and AP English III teacher at Texas High School in Texarkana where she served as department chair. She has been in education for 20 years and has taught grades seven through twelve. She has served as adjunct professor at LeMoyne-Owen College and Texarkana College.

Monica became Texas State Teacher of the Year in 2014, and she continues to travel the country speaking to teachers and advocating for the profession. She serves in the Texas State Teachers Association and the National Network of State Teachers of the Year. In addition, Monica is a 2015 Lowell Milken Center Fellow, and she will work with her students and the center to discover and honor unsung heroes. She is also a 2015 NEA Foundation Global Fellow. Monica is currently pursuing a doctorate of education in teacher leadership.

Tommy Young
First and Second Grade Educator
Waitsfield, VT
NEA Foundation Global Learning Fellow, Class of 2013

Tommy Young is a 1st and second grade teacher at Waitsfield Elementary School, in Waitsfield, Vermont. He is currently in his 21st year of teaching. He started his teaching career teaching first grade in the Northern Marianas Islands, on the island of Saipan. Along with his classroom teaching position, he was an adjunct professor at Champlain College and is currently the Varsity Girls' Basketball coach at Harwood Union High School. He was a part of the NEA/Better Lesson Master Teacher Project (Both Math and Science).

Tommy was a 2011 recipient of University of Vermont's Outstanding Teacher Award. In 2012, he was the recipient of the Vermont NEA Excellence in Teaching Award. He is also an NEA Foundation Awards for Teaching Excellence recipient and a 2013 Global Learning Fellow. In January of 2014, Tommy received the Sontag Prize in Urban Education. He